ARIANA GRANDE
FOR EASY PIANO

ISBN 978-1-5400-5085-4

Visit Hal Leonard Online at
www.halleonard.com

Contact us:
Hal Leonard
7777 West Bluemound Road
Milwaukee, WI 53213
Email: info@halleonard.com

In Europe, contact:
Hal Leonard Europe Limited
42 Wigmore Street
Marylebone, London, W1U 2RN
Email: info@halleonardeurope.com

In Australia, contact:
Hal Leonard Australia Pty. Ltd.
4 Lentara Court
Cheltenham, Victoria, 3192 Australia
Email: info@halleonard.com.au

CONTENTS

BREAK FREE

Words and Music by SAVAN KOTECHA,
MAX MARTIN and ANTON ZASLAVSKI

Moderate Dance groove

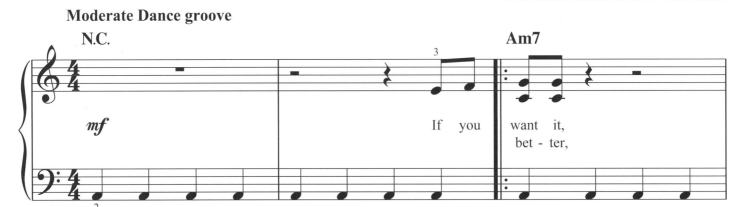

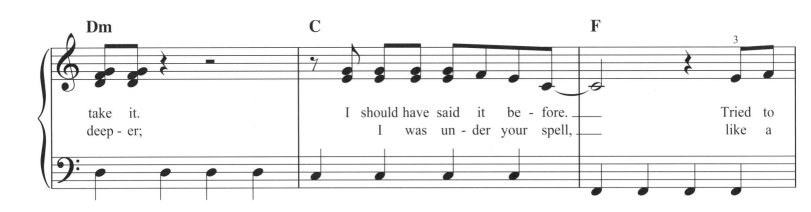

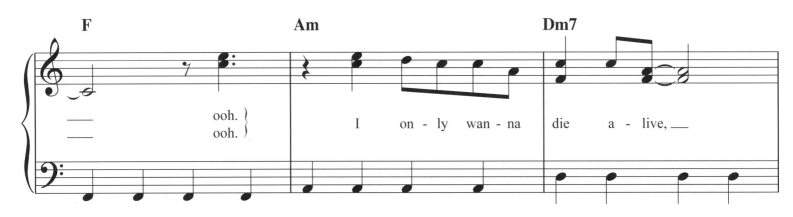

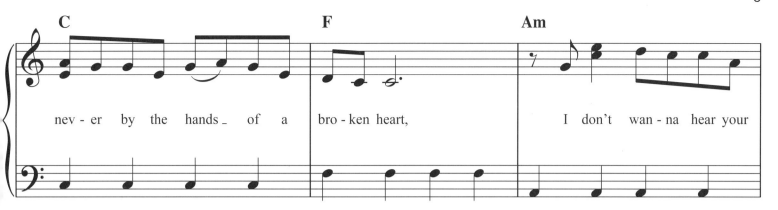

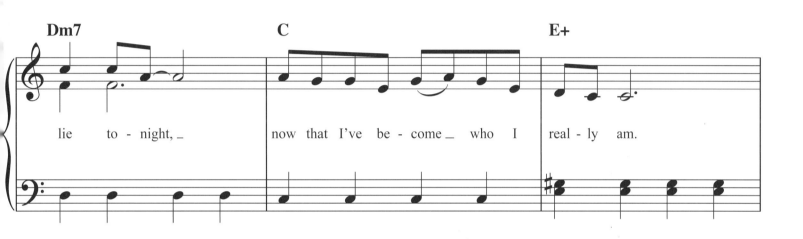

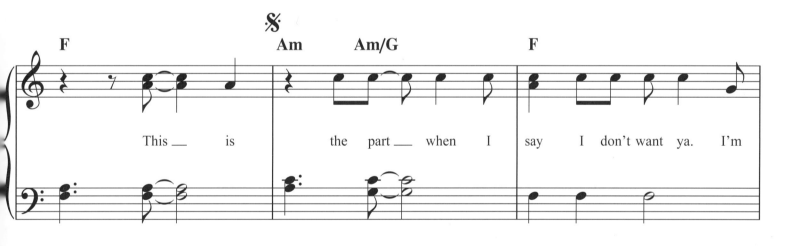

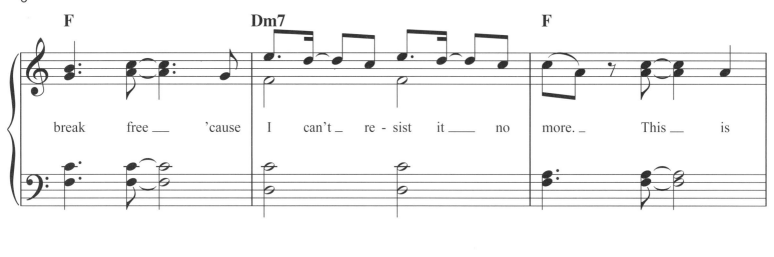

break free ___ 'cause I can't ___ re - sist it ___ no more. ___ This ___ is

the part ___ when I say I don't want ya. I'm strong - er than I've been be -

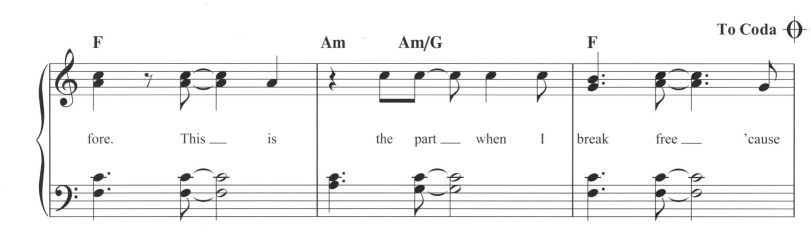

fore. This ___ is the part ___ when I break free ___ 'cause

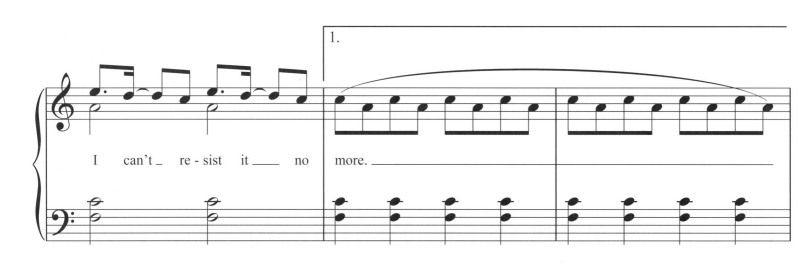

I can't ___ re - sist it ___ no more. ___

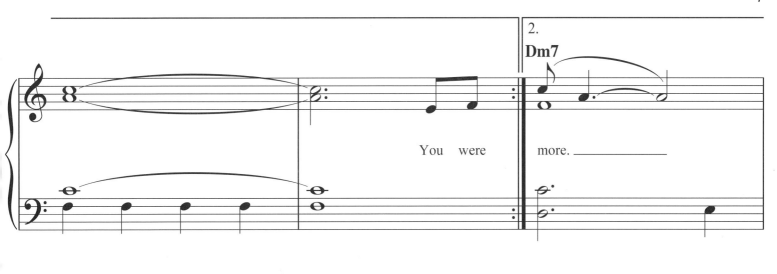

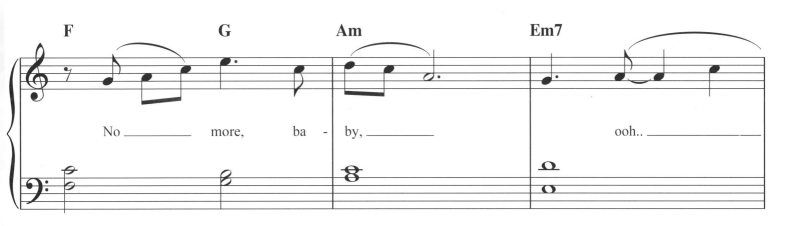

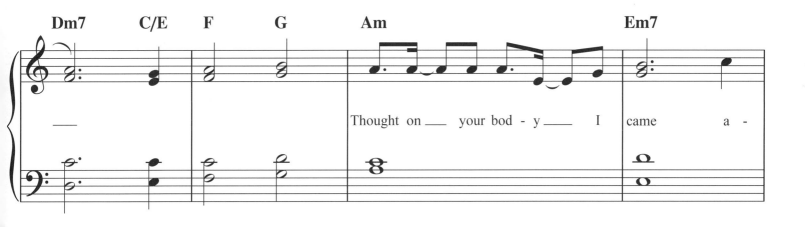

dreams it felt so _____ right, ___ but I woke up _____ ev - 'ry

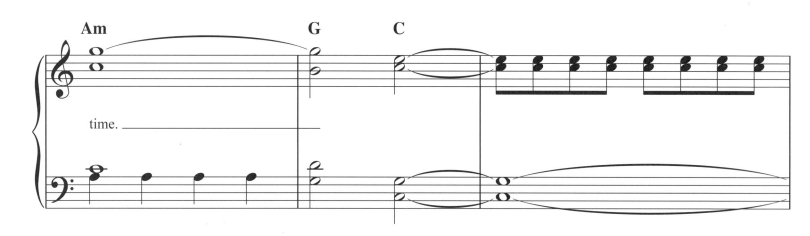

time. _____

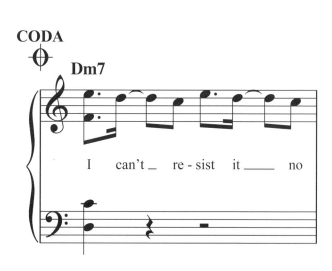

This ___ is

I can't ___ re - sist it _____ no

more. _____

BANG BANG
(Rap Version)

Words and Music by ONIKA MARAJ,
MAX MARTIN, SAVAN KOTECHA
and RICKARD GÖRANSSON

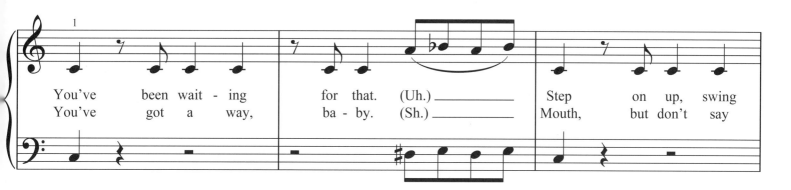

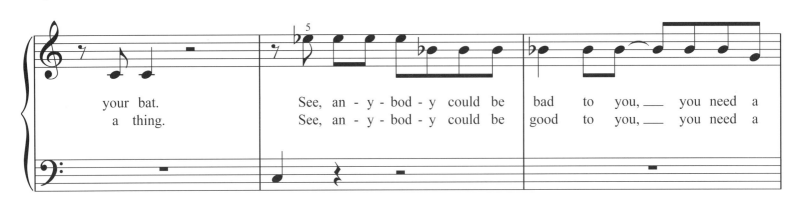

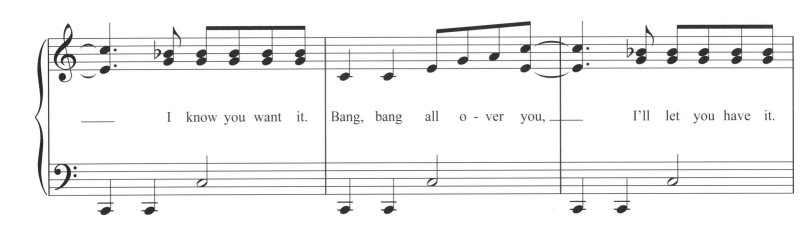

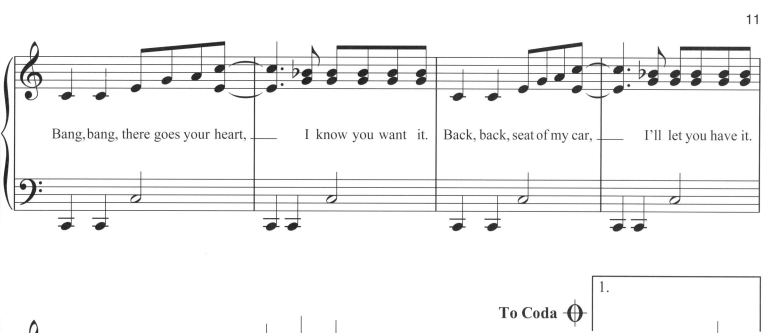

Bang, bang, there goes your heart, ___ I know you want it. Back, back, seat of my car, ___ I'll let you have it.

To Coda ⊕

1.

Wait a min-ute, let me take you there. Wait a min-ute, tell you, ah, hey!

2.

N.C.

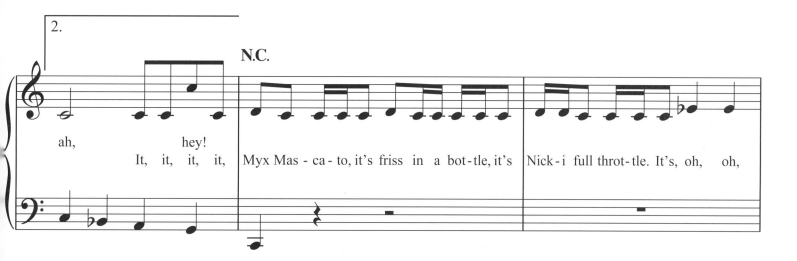

ah, hey! It, it, it, it, Myx Mas-ca-to, it's friss in a bot-tle, it's Nick-i full throt-tle. It's, oh, oh,

swim-min' in the grot-to, we win it in the lot-to, we dip-pin' in the pot of blue for sure.

Kit - ten so good, it's drip - pin' on wood, get a ride in the en - gine that could go.

Bat - man rob - bin' it; bang, bang, cock - in' it. Queen Nick - i dom - in - ant, prom - i - nent. It's me,

Jes - sie, and A - ri. If they test me, they sor - ry. Ride us up like a Har - ley, then pull off

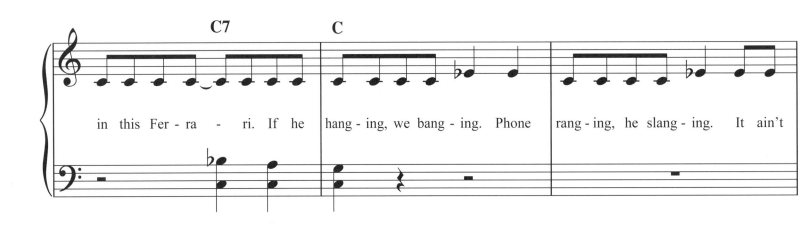

in this Fer - ra - ri. If he hang - ing, we bang - ing. Phone rang - ing, he slang - ing. It ain't

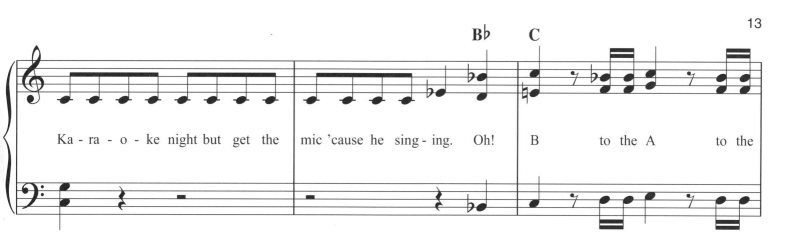

Ka - ra - o - ke night but get the mic 'cause he sing - ing. Oh! B to the A to the

N to the G to the uh. B to the A to the N to the G to the, hey.

N.C.

___ See, an - y - bod - y could be good to you. ___ You need a bad girl to blow your ___ mind, ___

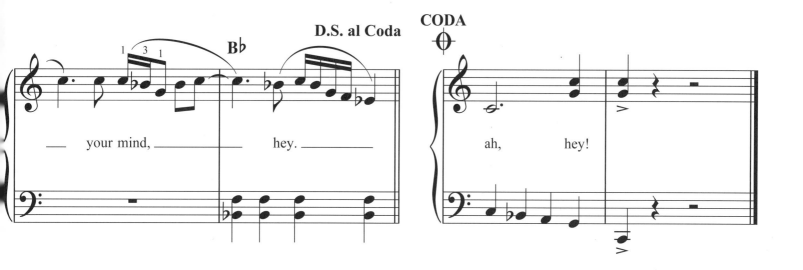

D.S. al Coda   CODA

___ your mind, _____ hey. _____ ah,   hey!

BREATHIN

Words and Music by ARIANA GRANDE,
SAVAN KOTECHA, MAX MARTIN
and ILYA

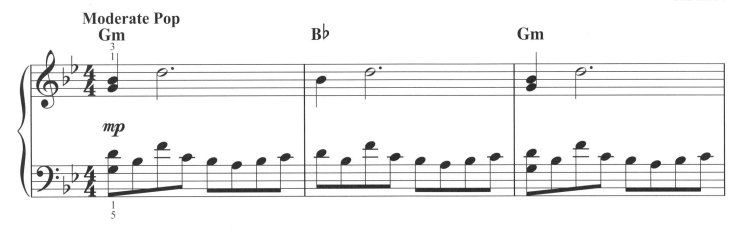

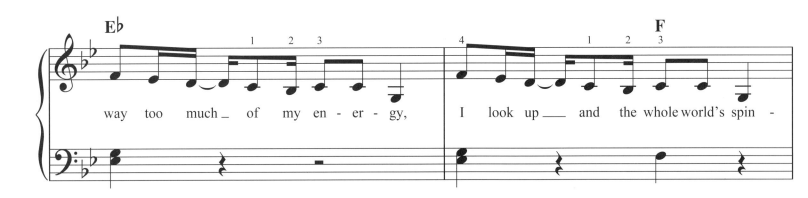

peo-ple tell ___ me to med - i - cate. Feel my blood run - ning, ___ swear the sky's fall-ing.

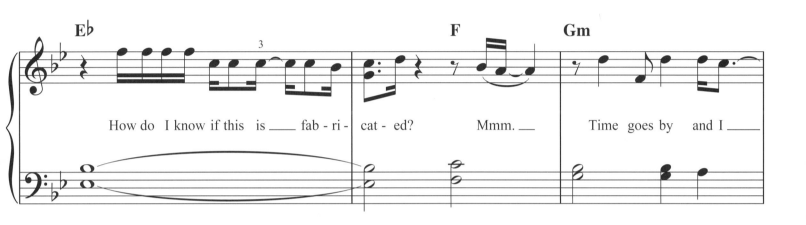

How do I know if this is ___ fab - ri - cat - ed? Mmm. ___ Time goes by and I ___

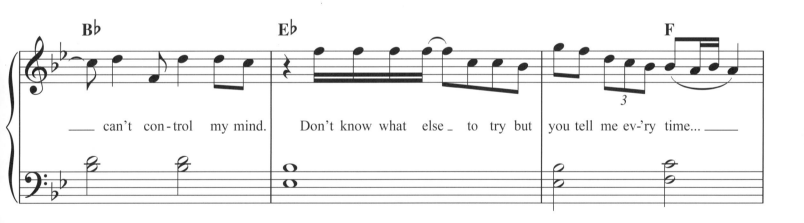

___ can't con-trol my mind. Don't know what else _ to try but you tell me ev-'ry time... ___

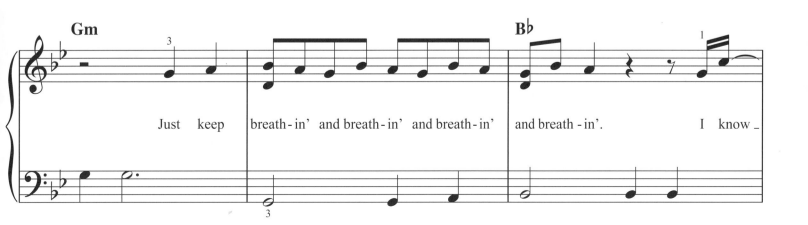

Just keep breath-in' and breath-in' and breath-in' and breath-in'. I know _

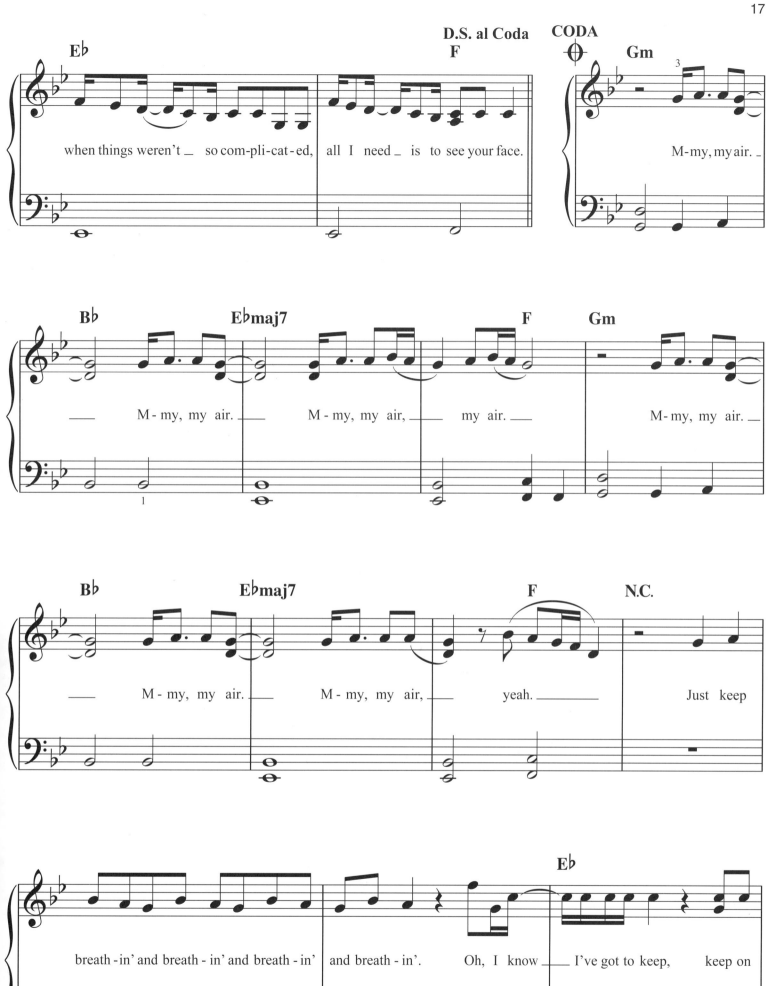

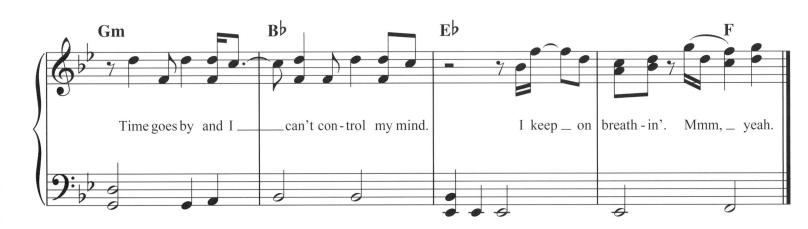

GOD IS A WOMAN

Words and Music by ARIANA GRANDE,
RICKARD GÖRANSSON, MAX MARTIN,
SAVAN KOTECHA and ILYA

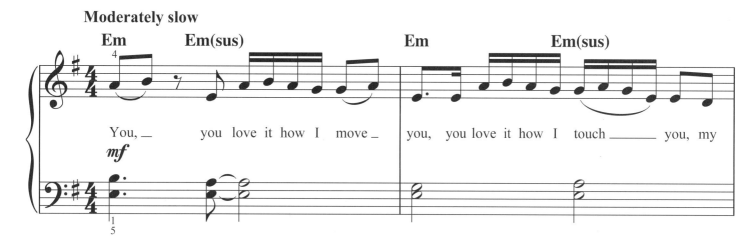

To Coda

one. _____ It lin-gers when it's done, you'll be-lieve God is a wom - an. _____

I don't wan-na waste no time, yeah, you ain't got a one track mind, yeah.

Have it an-y way you like, yeah and I can tell that you know I know how I want it.

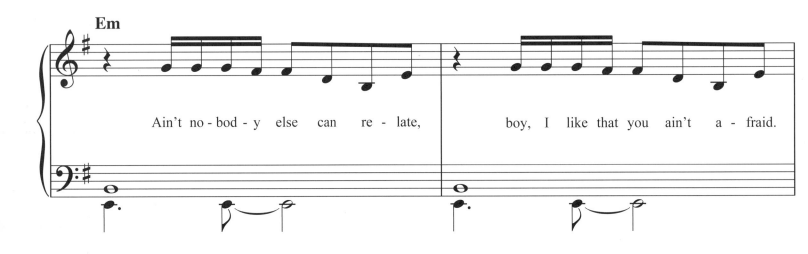

Ain't no-bod-y else can re-late, boy, I like that you ain't a-fraid.

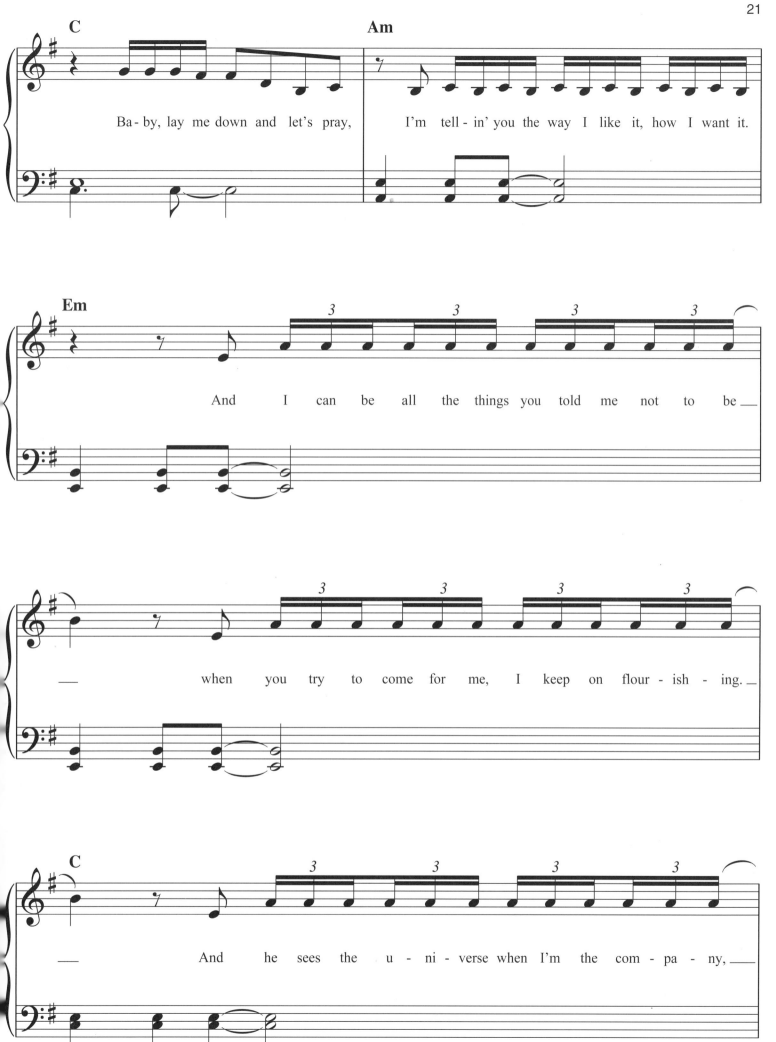

D.C. al Coda

CODA

Am

_____ it's all in me.

Em

I'll tell you all the things you should know

so, ba-by, take my hand, save your soul.

C

We can make it last, take it slow _____

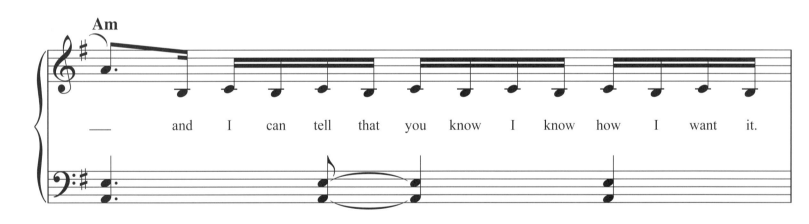

Am

_____ and I can tell that you know I know how I want it.

Em

But you're dif-f'rent from the rest and, boy, if you con-fess, you might get blessed.

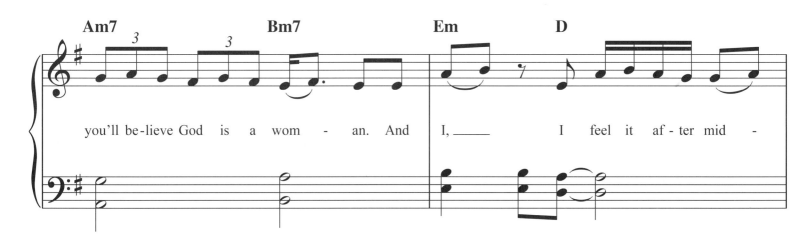

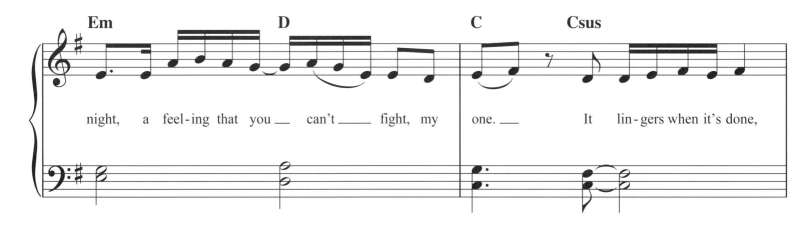

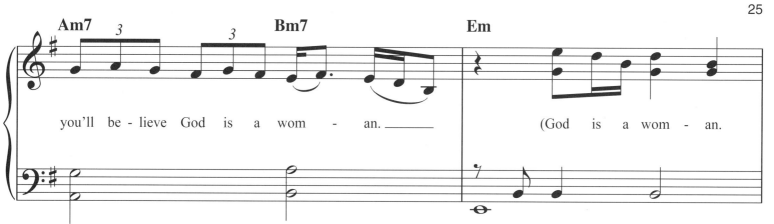

you'll be-lieve God is a wom - an. _____ (God is a wom - an.

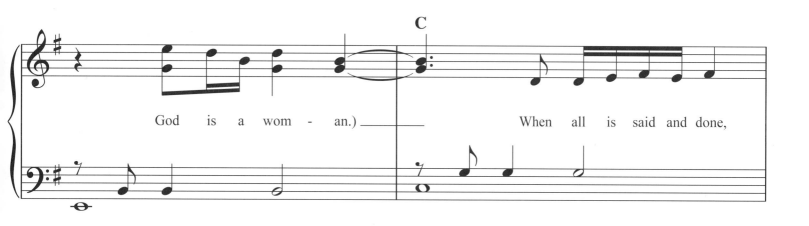

God is a wom - an.) _____ When all is said and done,

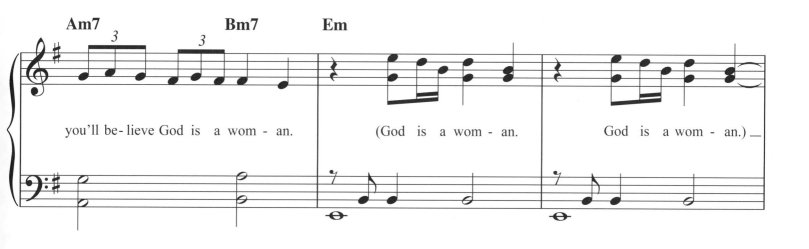

you'll be-lieve God is a wom - an. (God is a wom - an. God is a wom - an.) _

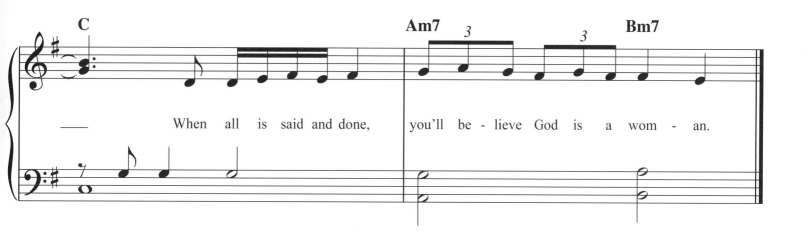

_____ When all is said and done, you'll be-lieve God is a wom - an.

DANGEROUS WOMAN

Words and Music by MAX MARTIN,
JOHAN CARLSSON and ROSS GOLAN

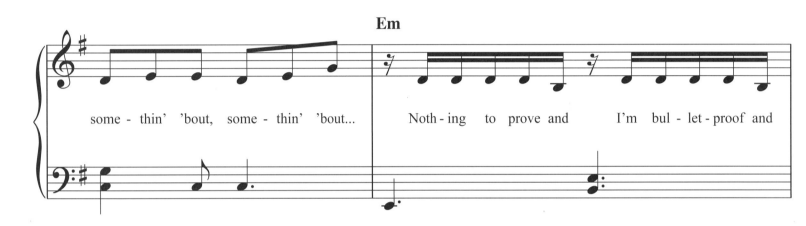

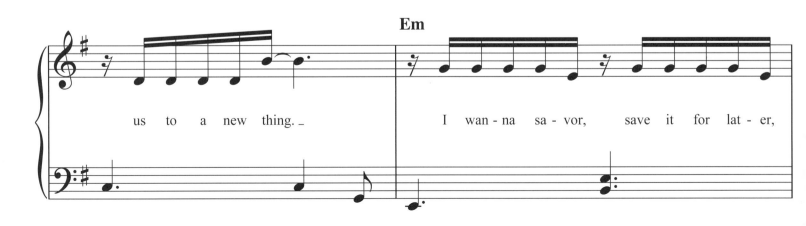

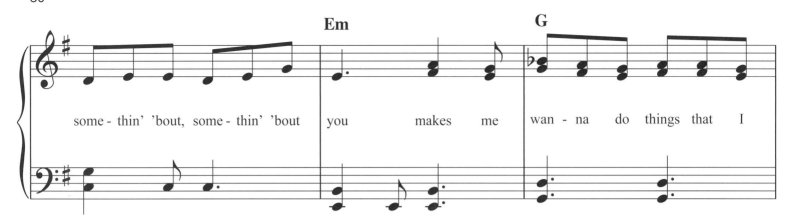

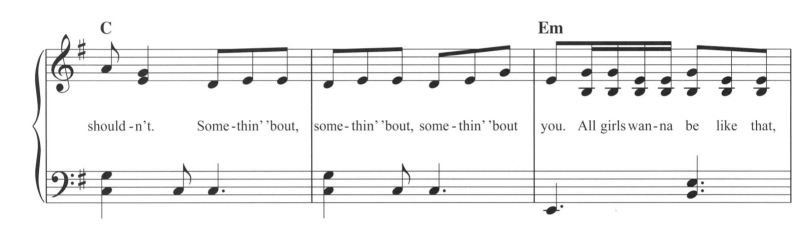

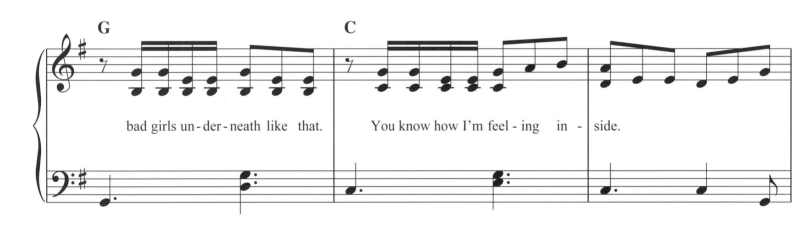

INTO YOU

Words and Music by ILYA, SAVAN KOTECHA,
MAX MARTIN, ARIANA GRANDE
and ALEXANDER KRONLUND

Moderate dance groove

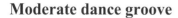

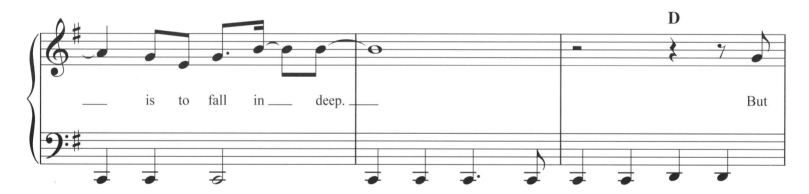

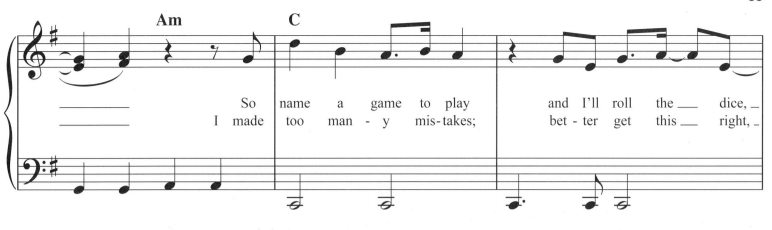

So name a game to play
I made too man - y mis - takes;

and I'll roll the __ dice, __
bet - ter get this __ right, __

hey.
hey.

Oh, ba - by, look what you start - ed. The

tem - per - 'ture's ris - in' in here. Is

this gon - na hap - pen? Been wait - in' and wait - in' for you to

make a move __ (ooh) __

be - fore I make a move __ (ooh). __

So ba-by, come light me up and may-be I'll let you on it. ___ A

lit -tle bit dan - ger -ous, but, ba-by, that's how I want it. ___ A

lit -tle less con - ver - sa - tion and a lit -tle more touch my bod - y ___ 'cause

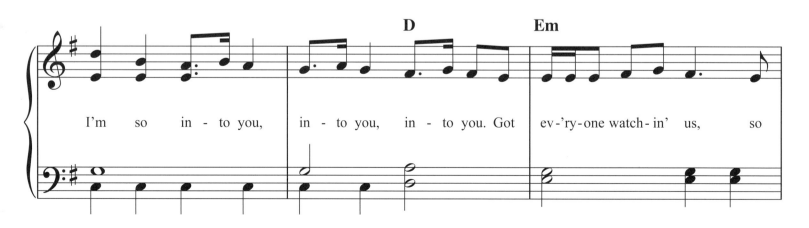

I'm so in - to you, in - to you, in - to you. Got ev -'ry-one watch-in' us, so

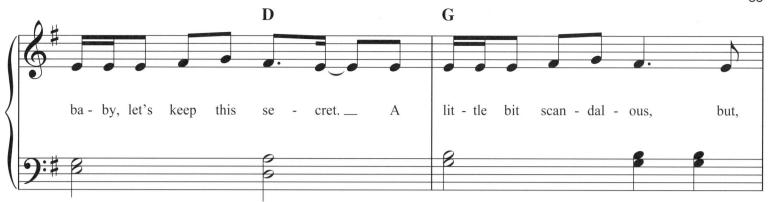

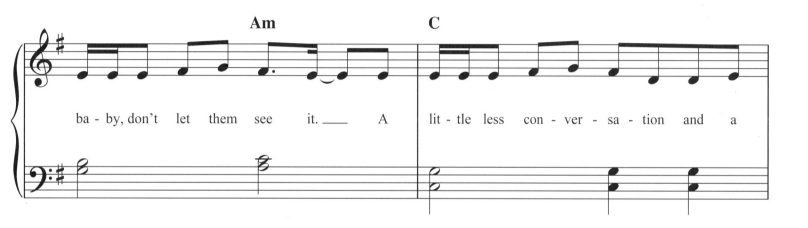

CODA

into you, in - to you. So, come light me up. ___

A lit - tle dan - ger - ous. ___ A

lit - tle less con - ver - sa - tion ___ and a lit - tle more touch my bod - y, ___ 'cause

I'm so in - to you, in - to you, in - to you.

ONE LAST TIME

Words and Music by DAVID GUETTA,
SAVAN KOTECHA, GIORGIO TUINFORT,
CARL FALK and RAMI YACOUB

Moderate Dance groove

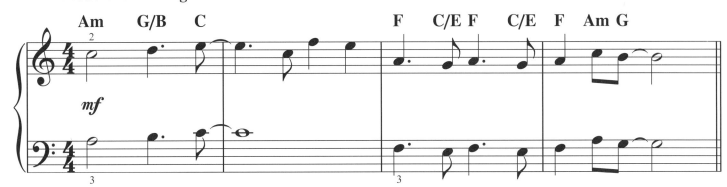

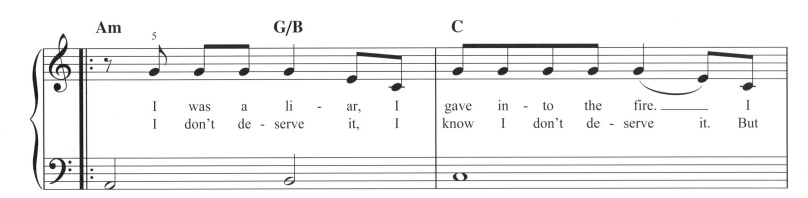

I was a li - ar, I gave in - to the fire. ___ I
I don't de - serve it, I know I don't de - serve it. But

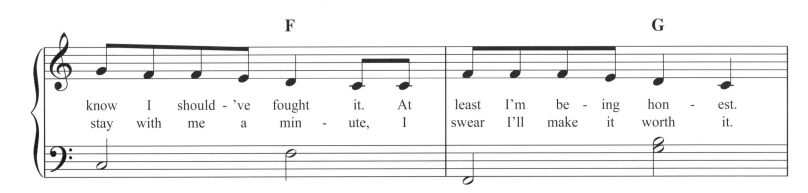

know I should - 've fought it. At least I'm be - ing hon - est.
stay with me a min - ute, I swear I'll make it worth it.

Feel like a fail - ure 'cause I know that I failed you. I
Can't you for - give me, at least just tem - po - rar - 'ly. I

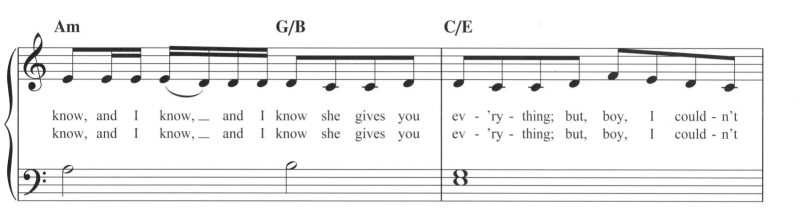

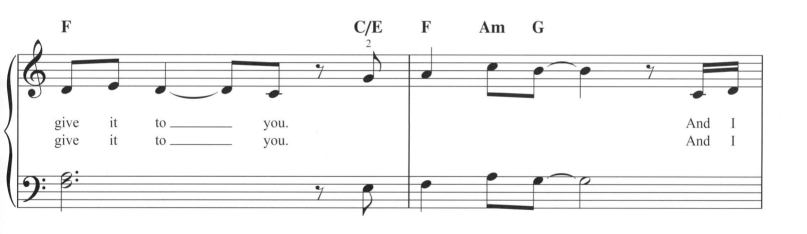

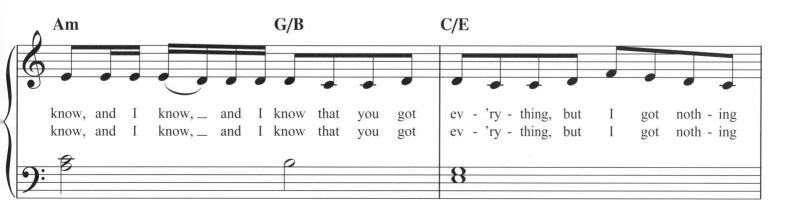

here with - out _____ ya.
here with - out _____ you, ba - by.
So, one last time, _

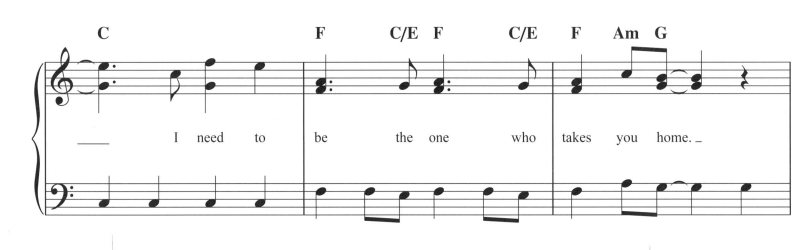

_____ I need to be the one who takes you home. _

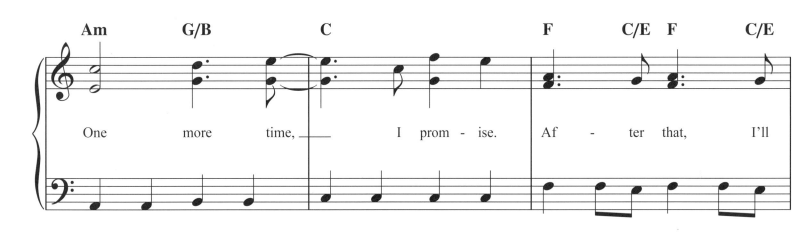

One more time, _____ I prom - ise. Af - ter that, I'll

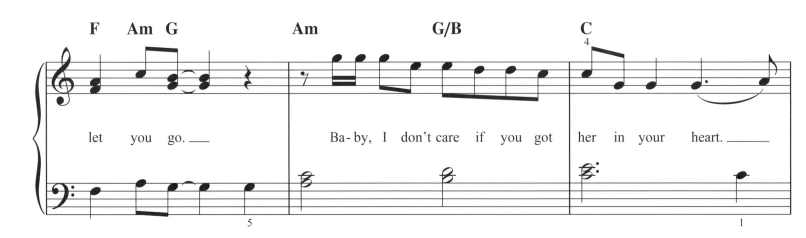

let you go. _____ Ba - by, I don't care if you got her in your heart. _____

All I real-ly care is you wake up in my arms. One last time,

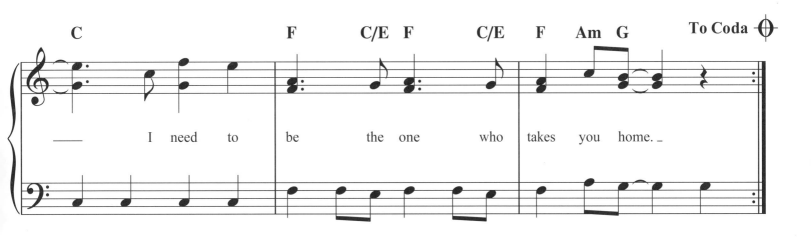

I need to be the one who takes you home.

To Coda ⊕

I know I should-'ve fought it. At

least I'm be-ing hon-est, yeah. Just

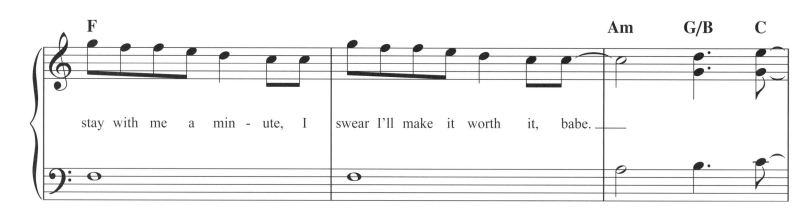

stay with me a min - ute, I | swear I'll make it worth it, babe. ___

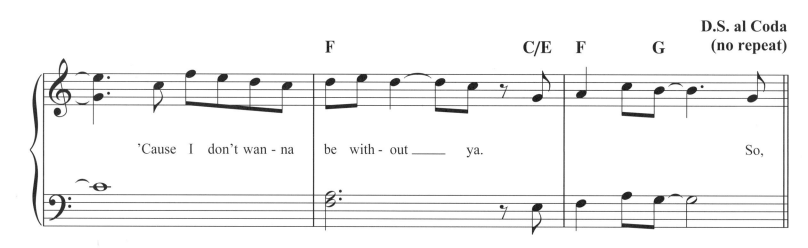

D.S. al Coda
(no repeat)

'Cause I don't wan - na | be with - out ___ ya. | So,

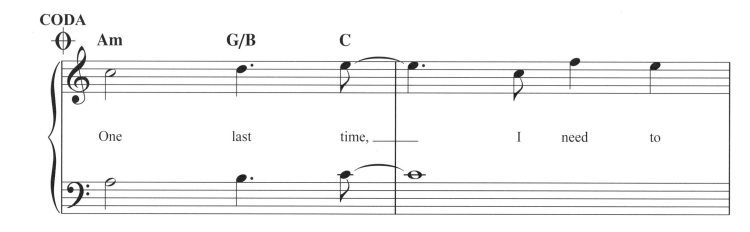

CODA

One last time, ___ | I need to

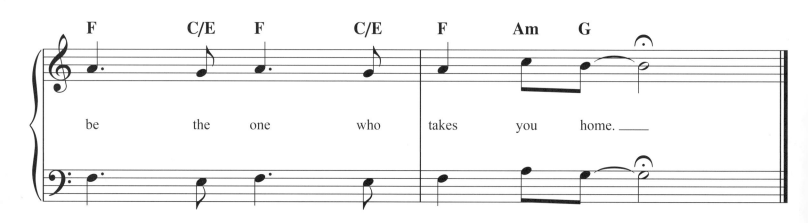

be the one who | takes you home. ___

LOVE ME HARDER

Words and Music by ABEL TESFAYE,
MAX MARTIN, SAVAN KOTECHA,
ANDERS SVENSSON, AHMAD BALSHE
and ALI PAYAMI

Moderate Dance beat

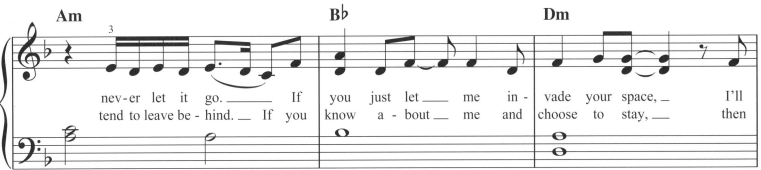

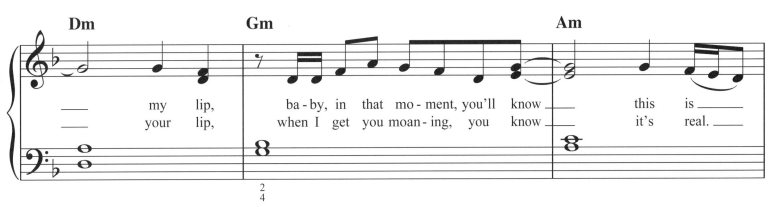

Ooh, _____ ooh, _____ ooh, ___ ooh, _____ love me, love me, love me. __

Ooh, _____ ooh, _____ ooh, ___ ooh, _____ hard - er, hard - er, hard - er. I

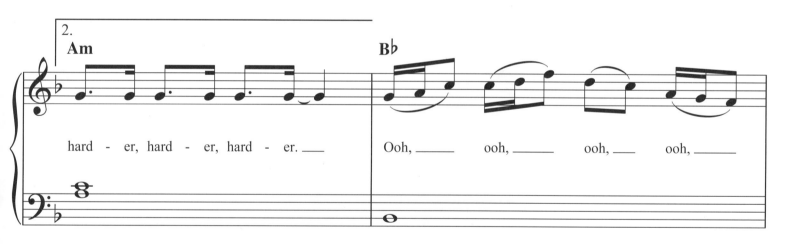

hard - er, hard - er, hard - er. __ Ooh, _____ ooh, _____ ooh, ___ ooh, _____

love me, love me, love me. __ Ooh, __ ooh, __ ooh, _ ooh, __ hard - er, hard - er, hard - er. __

So, what do I do if I can't fig-ure it out? ___ { You've got to / I'm gon - na

1. try, try, try a - gain. ___

2. leave, leave, leave a-gain. If you want to keep ___ me, you

got to, got ___ to, got to, got to, got to love me hard - er. I will

love you, love ___ you, love... And if you real - ly need ___ me, you

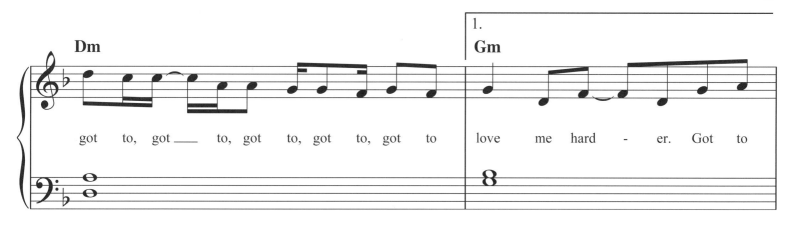

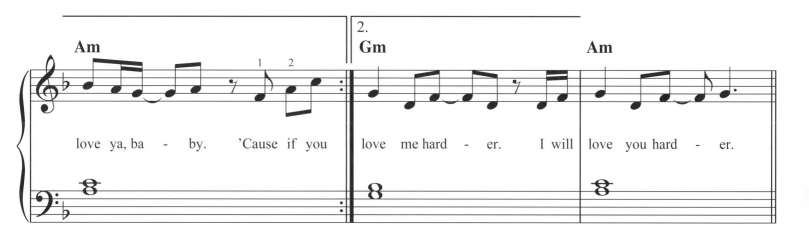

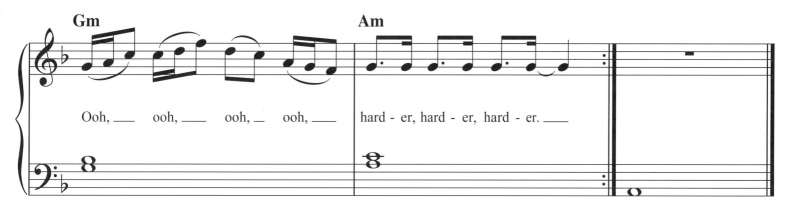

7 RINGS

Words and Music by RICHARD RODGERS,
OSCAR HAMMERSTEIN II, ARIANA GRANDE,
VICTORIA McCANTS, KIMBERLY KRYSIUK,
TAYLA PARX, TOMMY BROWN,
NJOMZA VITIA, MICHAEL FOSTER
and CHARLES ANDERSON

Slow, half-time groove

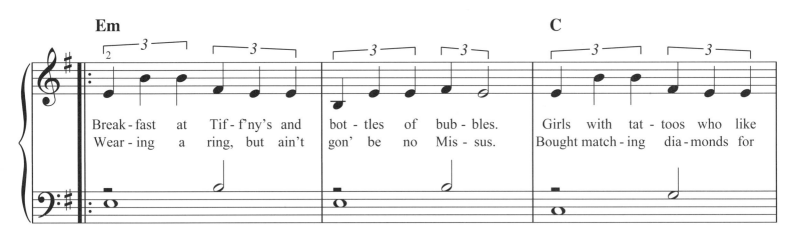

Break - fast at Tif - f'ny's and bot - tles of bub - bles.
Wear - ing a ring, but ain't gon' be no Mis - sus.

Girls with tat - toos who like
Bought match - ing dia - monds for

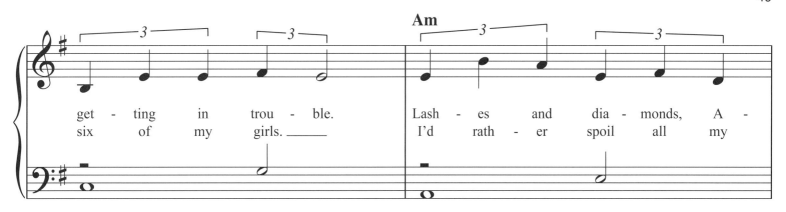

getting in trou-ble.
six of my girls. _____

Am

Lash - es and dia - monds, A -
I'd rath - er spoil all my

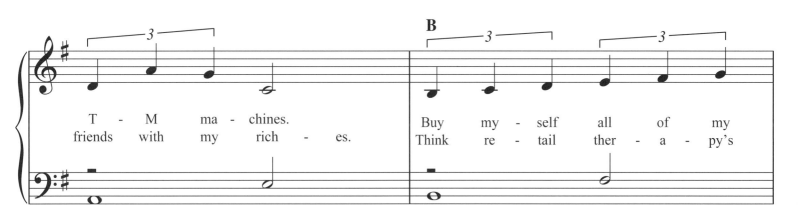

T - M ma - chines.
friends with my rich - es.

B

Buy my - self all of my
Think re - tail ther - a - py's

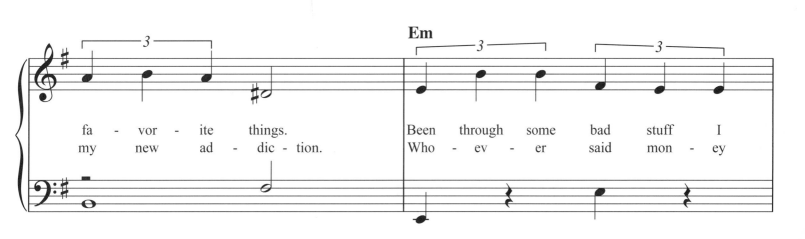

fa - vor - ite things.
my new ad - dic - tion.

Em

Been through some bad stuff I
Who - ev - er said mon - ey

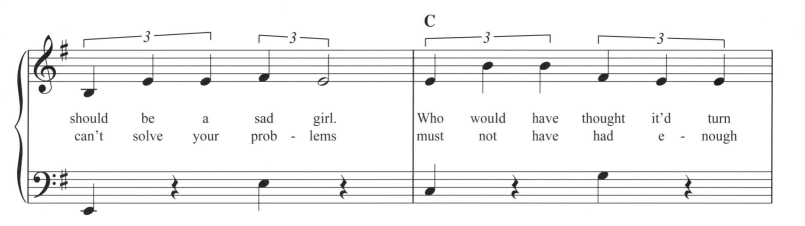

should be a sad girl.
can't solve your prob - lems

C

Who would have thought it'd turn
must not have had e - nough

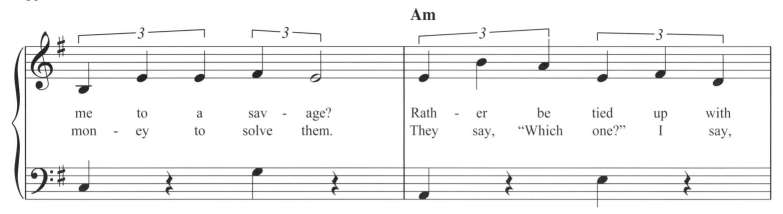

me to a sav - age?
mon - ey to solve them.

Rath - er be tied up with
They say, "Which one?" I say,

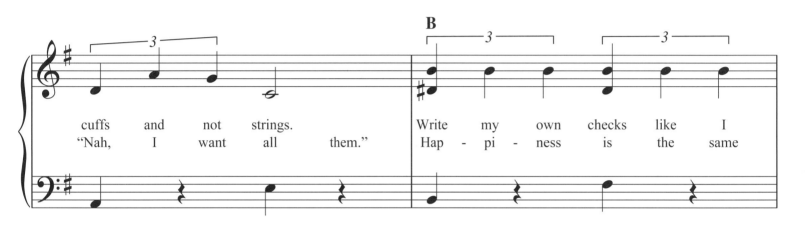

cuffs and not strings.
"Nah, I want all them."

Write my own checks like I
Hap - pi - ness is like the same

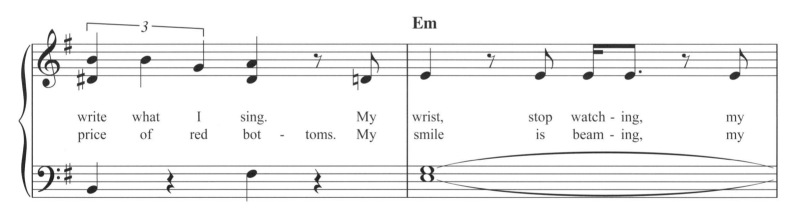

write what I sing. My
price of red bot - toms. My

wrist, stop watch - ing, my
smile is beam - ing, my

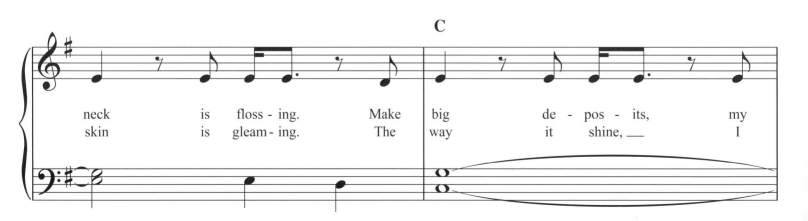

neck is floss - ing. Make
skin is gleam - ing. The

big de - pos - its, my
way it shine, __ I

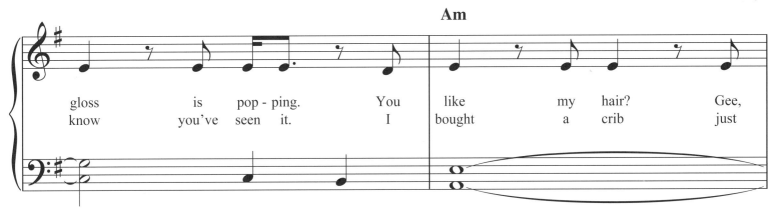

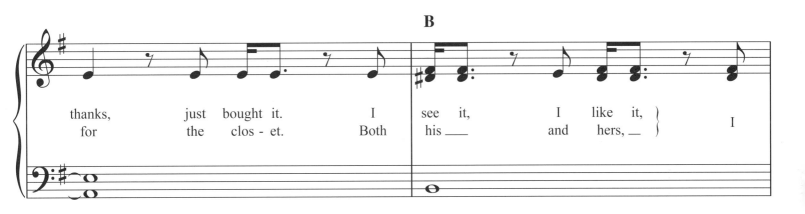

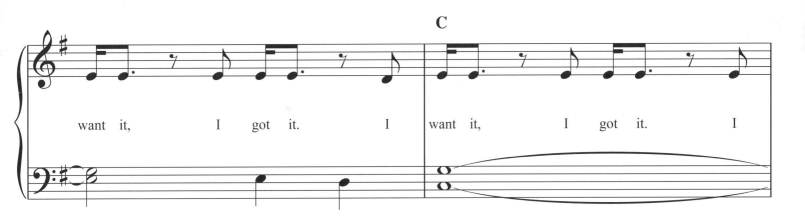

want it,   I got it.   You like   my hair?   Gee, thanks,   just bought it.   I

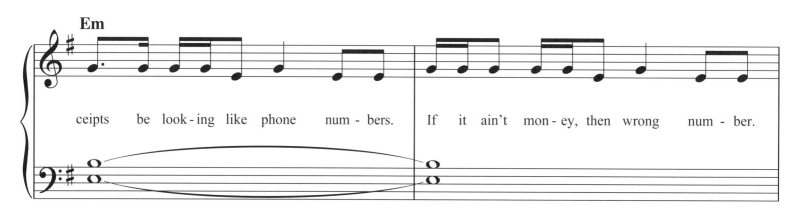

see it,   I like it,   I want it,   I got it, yeah.   want it,   I got it. My re-

ceipts be look-ing like phone num-bers.   If it ain't mon-ey, then wrong num-ber.

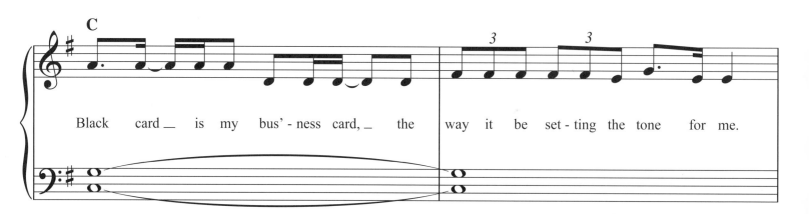

Black card _ is my bus'-ness card, _ the   way it be set-ting the tone for me.

Am

I don't mean to brag, but I be like, "Put it in the bag," yeah.

B   **Em**

When you see them racks, they stacked up like, _____ yeah. Shoot, go from the store to the booth,

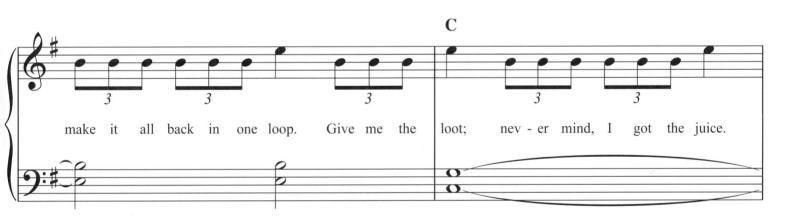

C

make it all back in one loop. Give me the loot; nev-er mind, I got the juice.

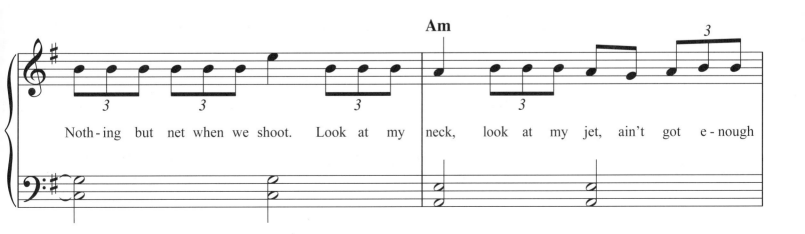

Am

Noth-ing but net when we shoot. Look at my neck, look at my jet, ain't got e-nough

mon - ey to pay me re - spect. Ain't no bud - get when I'm on the set. If I

N.C.

D.S. al Coda

like it, then that's what I get, yeah. I

CODA

like it, I got it, yeah.

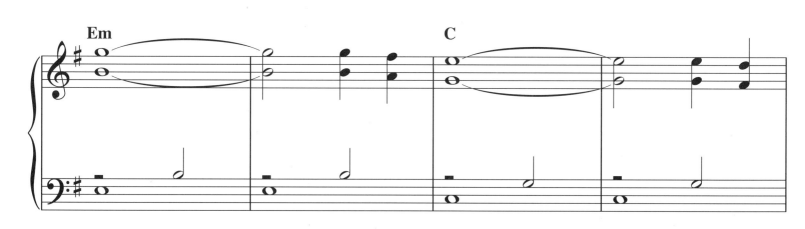

Em

C

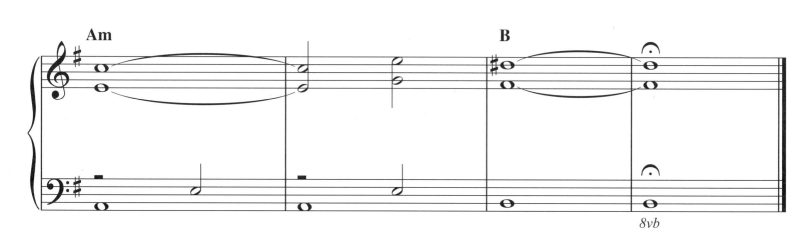

Am

B

8vb

NO TEARS LEFT TO CRY

Words and Music by ARIANA GRANDE,
SAVAN KOTECHA, MAX MARTIN
and ILYA

Atmospherically

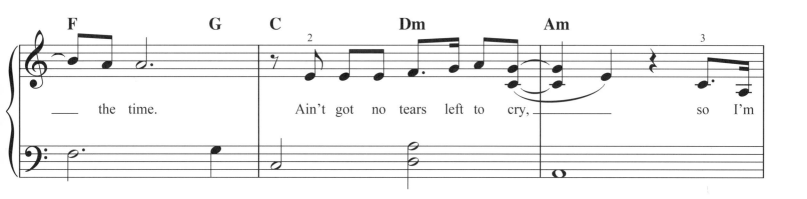

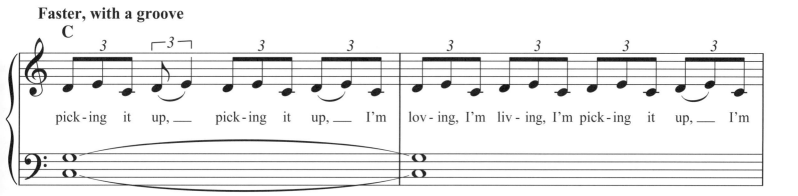

Faster, with a groove

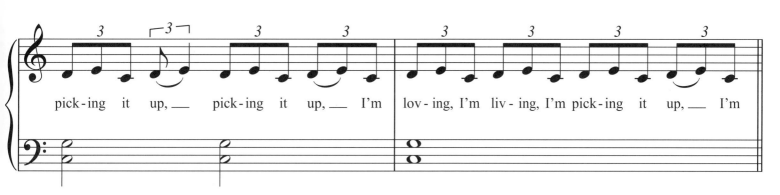

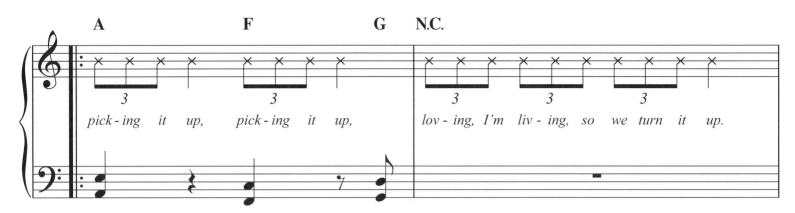

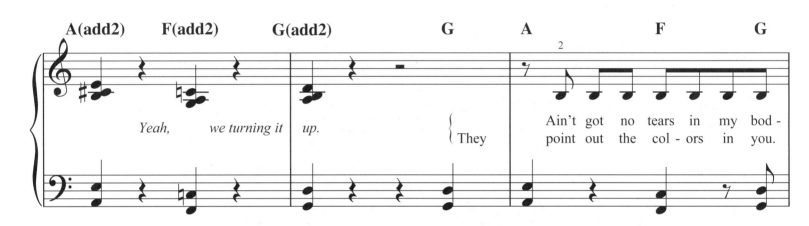

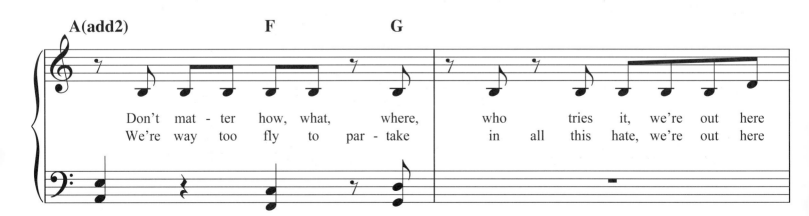

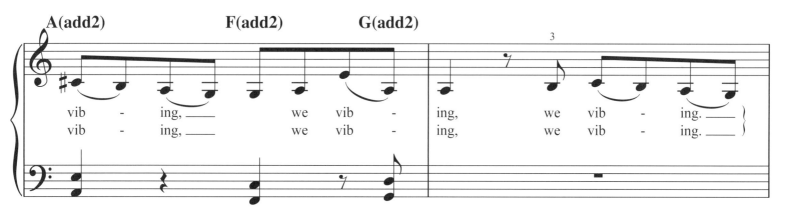

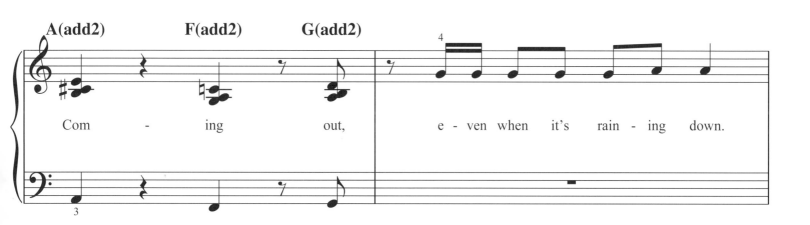

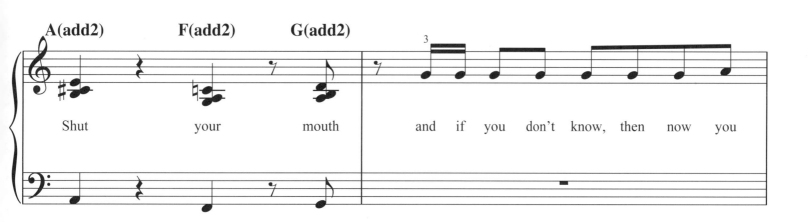

know it, babe, know it, babe, yeah. Right now, I'm in a state

of mind I wan-na be in, like, all the time.

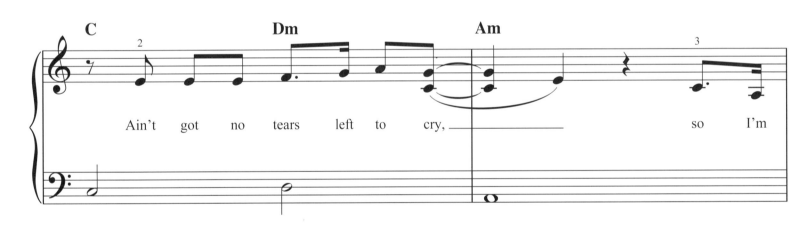

Ain't got no tears left to cry, so I'm

pick-ing it up, pick-ing it up, I'm lov-ing, I'm liv-ing, I'm pick-ing it up.

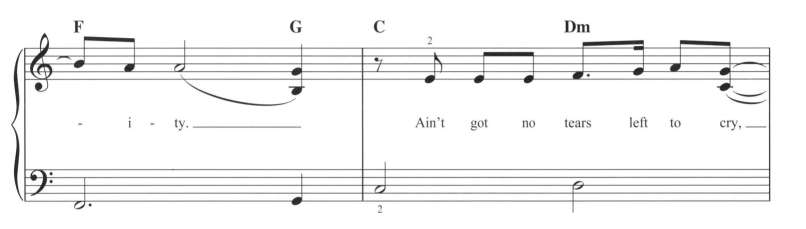

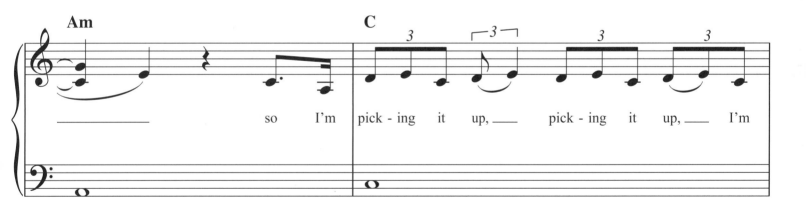

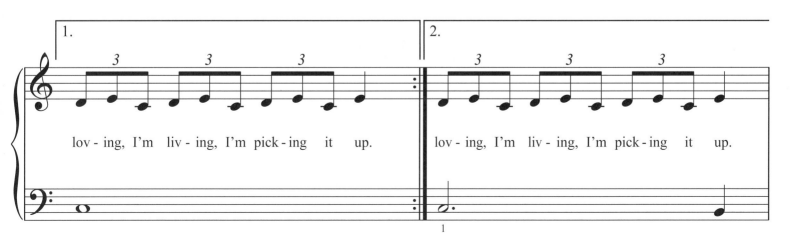

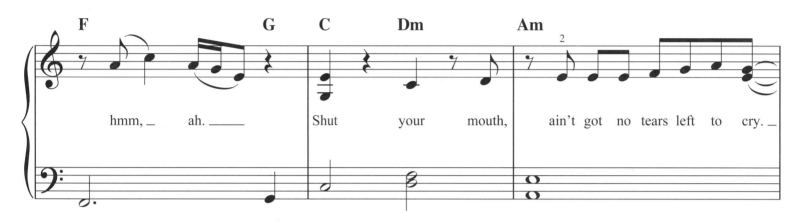

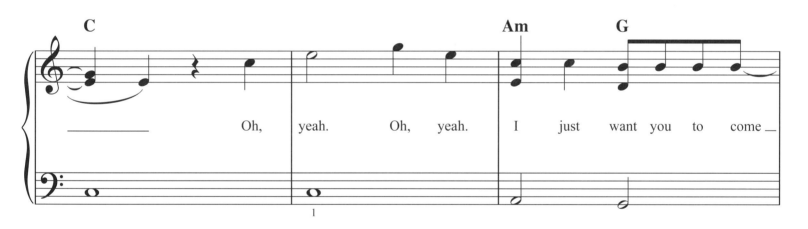

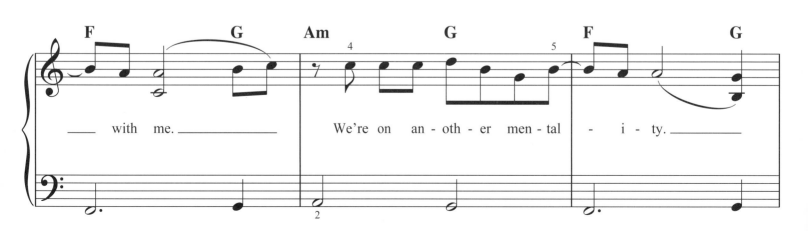

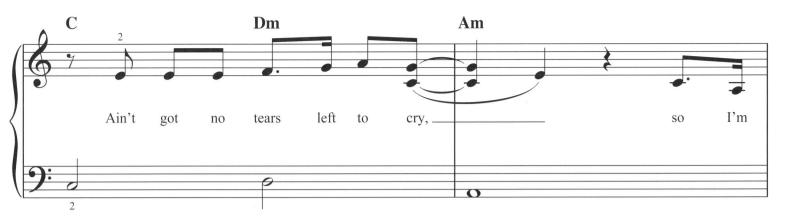

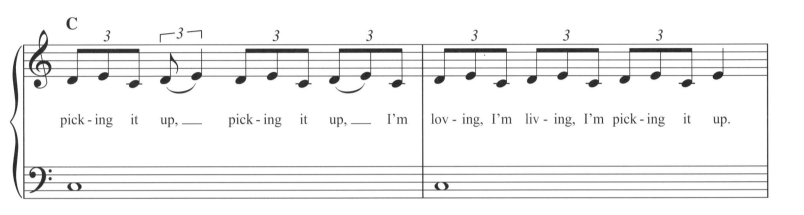

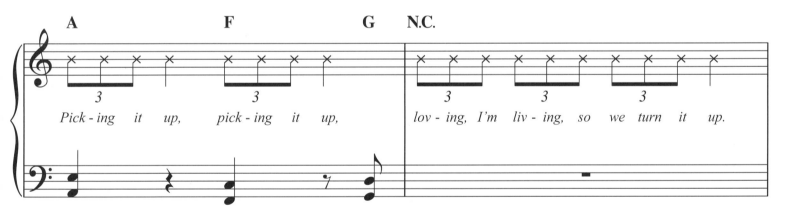

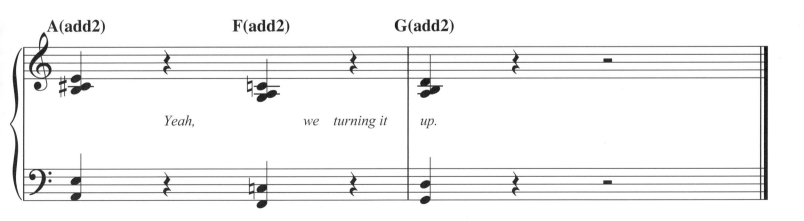

PROBLEM

Words and Music by ILYA,
ARIANA GRANDE, MAX MARTIN,
SAVAN KOTECHA and AMETHYST AMELIA KELLY

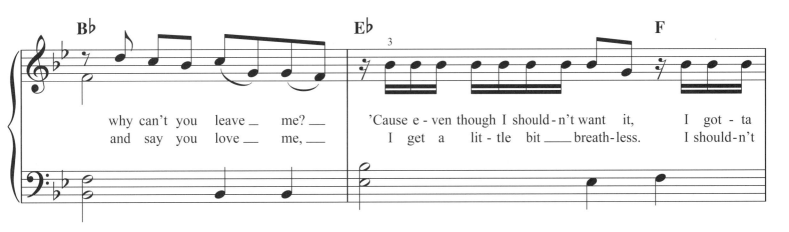

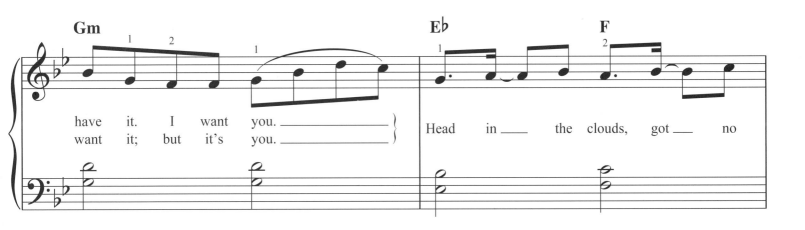

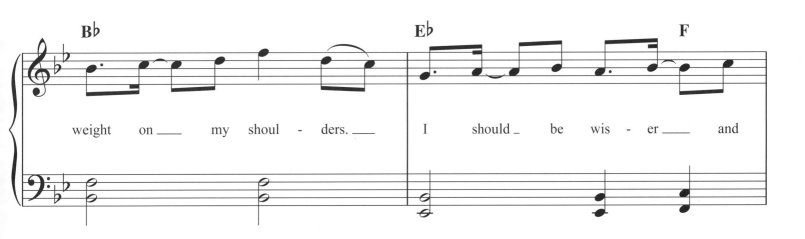

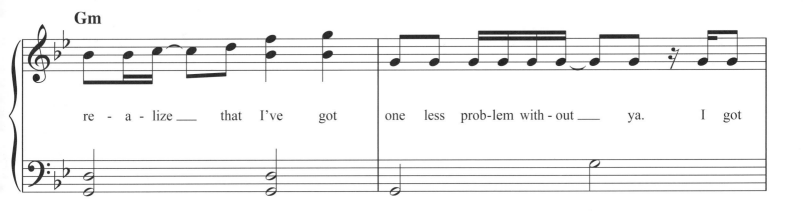

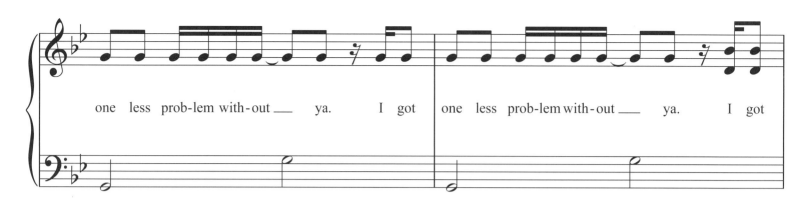

one less prob-lem with-out ___ ya. I got one less prob-lem with-out ___ ya. I got

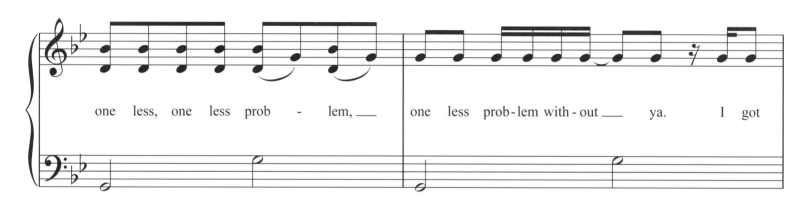

one less, one less prob - lem, ___ one less prob-lem with-out ___ ya. I got

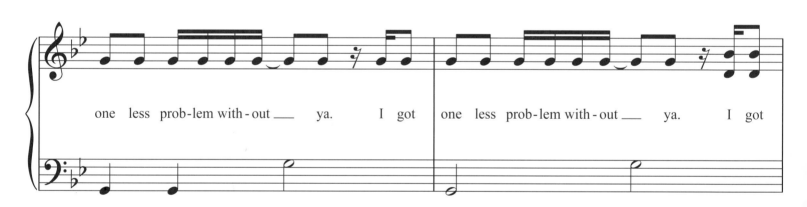

one less prob-lem with-out ___ ya. I got one less prob-lem with-out ___ ya. I got

N.C.

one less, one less prob - lem. ___

Rap: *(See additional lyrics)*

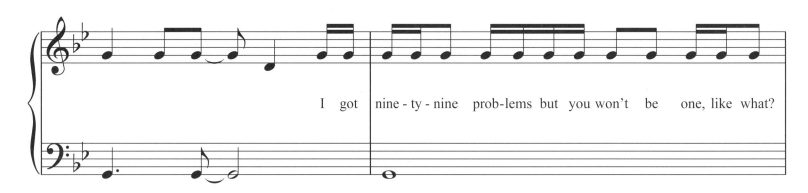

I got nine-ty-nine prob-lems but you won't be one, like what?

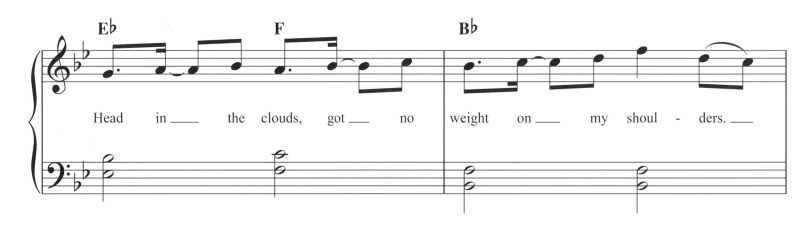

One less, one less prob - lem. _____

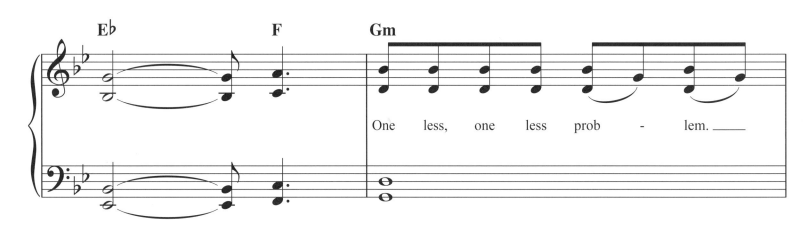

Head in _____ the clouds, got _____ no weight on _____ my shoul - ders. _____

I should _ be wis - er _____ and re - a - lize _____ that I've got,

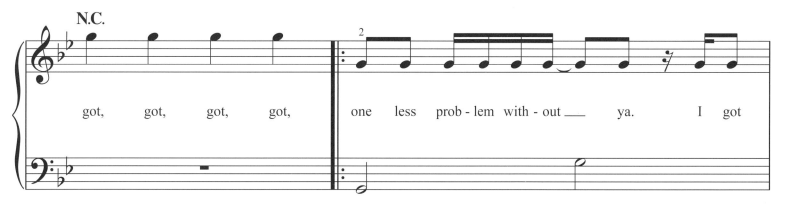

got, got, got, got, one less prob - lem with - out ___ ya. I got

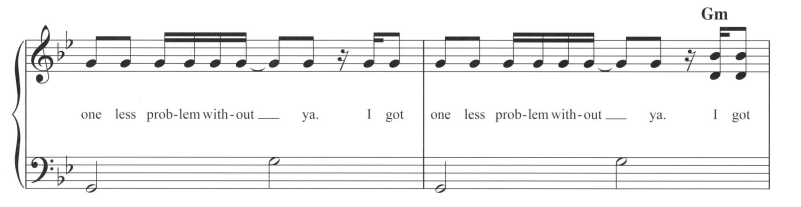

Gm

one less prob-lem with-out ___ ya. I got one less prob-lem with-out ___ ya. I got

1. one less, one less prob - lem, ___

2. one less, one less prob - lem. ___

Additional Lyrics

Rap: Smart money bettin' I'll be better off without you.
In no time I'll be forgettin' all about you.
You sayin' that you know, but I really, really doubt.
You understand? My life is easy when I ain't around you.
Iggy, Iggy too biggie to be here stressin'.
I'm thinkin' I love the thought of you more than I love your presence.
And the best thing now is probably for you to exit.
I let you go, let you back. I finally learned my lesson.
No half-steppin', either you want it or you just playin'.
I'm listenin' to you knowin' I can't believe what you're sayin'.
There's a million you's, baby boo, so don't be dumb.
(I got 99 problems but you won't be one, like what?)

SIDE TO SIDE

Words and Music by ARIANA GRANDE,
ONIKA MARAJ, ALEXANDER KRONLUND,
MAX MARTIN, SAVAN KOTECHA and ILYA

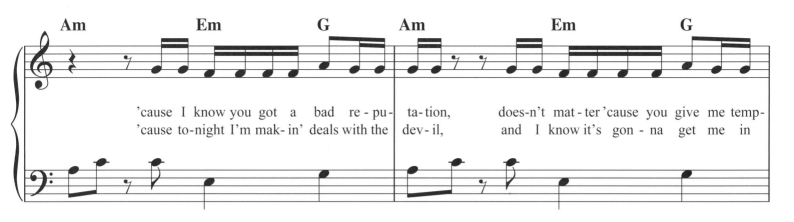

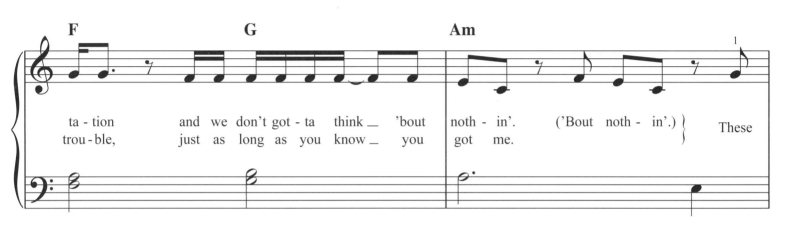

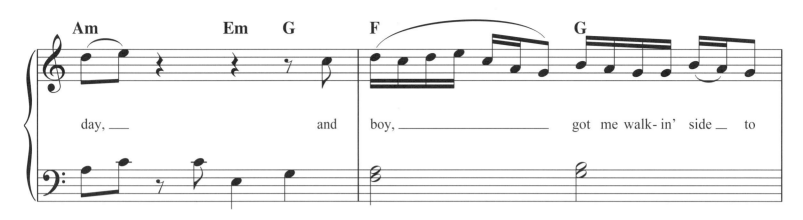

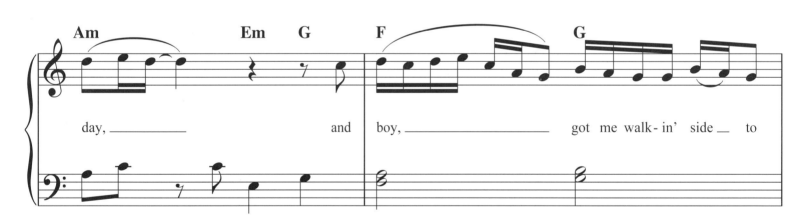

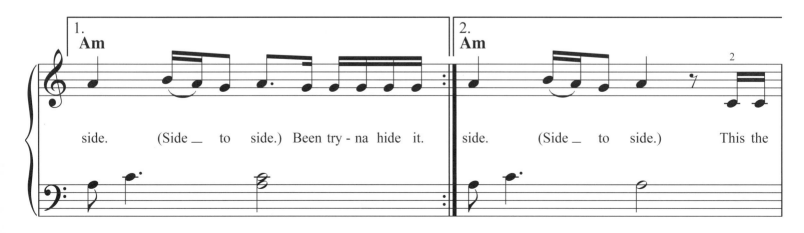

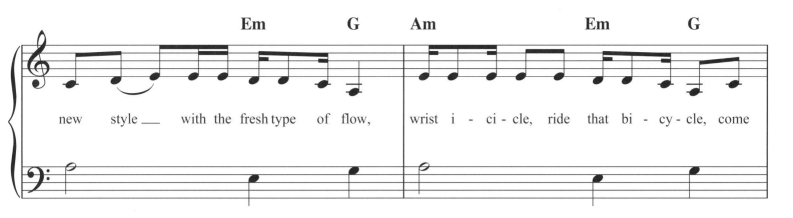

new style ___ with the fresh type of flow, wrist i - ci - cle, ride that bi - cy - cle, come

true yo, ___ get you this type of show. If you wan-na Mi - naj, I got a tri - cy - cle.

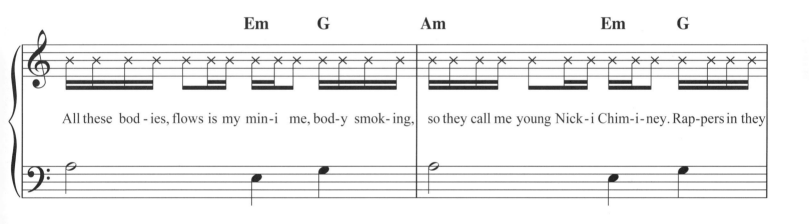

All these bod - ies, flows is my min-i me, bod-y smok-ing, so they call me young Nick-i Chim-i-ney. Rap-pers in they

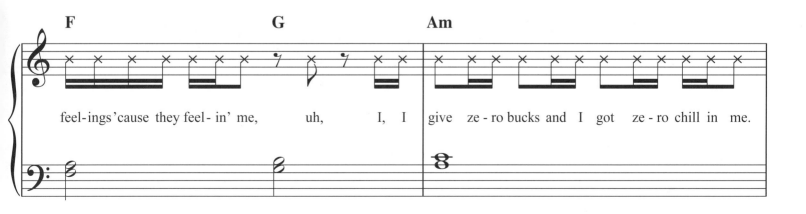

feel-ings 'cause they feel- in' me, uh, I, I give ze-ro bucks and I got ze-ro chill in me.

Kiss-in' me, copped the blue box __ that say Tif-fa-ny. Cur-ry with the shot, just tell 'em to call me Steph-a-nie.

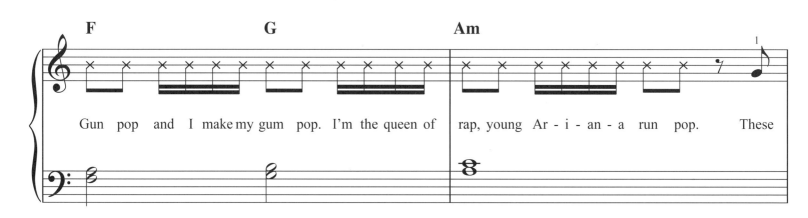

Gun pop and I make my gum pop. I'm the queen of rap, young Ar - i - an - a run pop. These

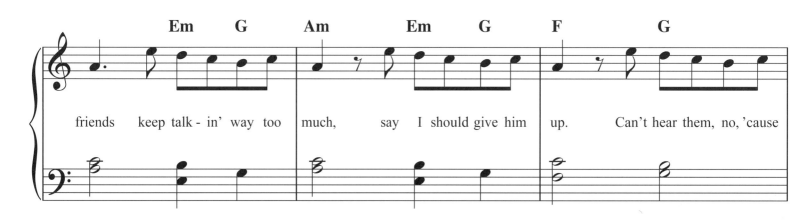

friends keep talk-in' way too much, say I should give him up. Can't hear them, no, 'cause

I... _____ I've been there all night, (Been there all night, ba - by.) I've been there all

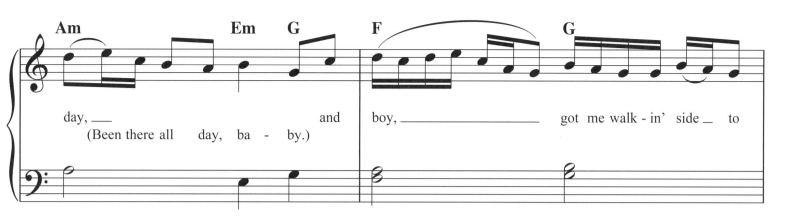

day, ____ and boy, _____ got me walk - in' side ____ to
(Been there all day, ba - by.)

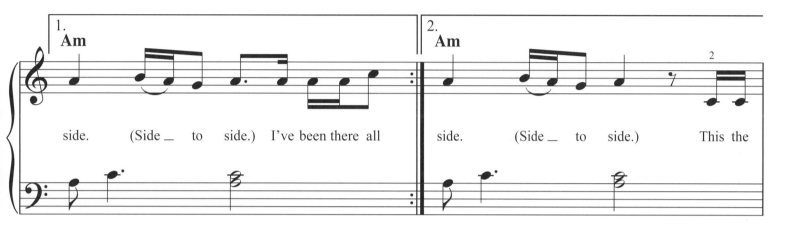

1.
side. (Side ____ to side.) I've been there all

2.
side. (Side ____ to side.) This the

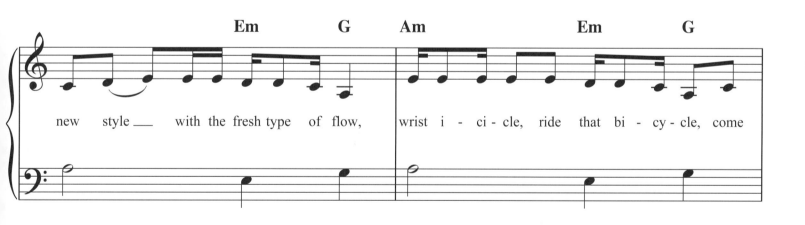

new style ____ with the fresh type of flow, wrist i - ci - cle, ride that bi - cy - cle, come

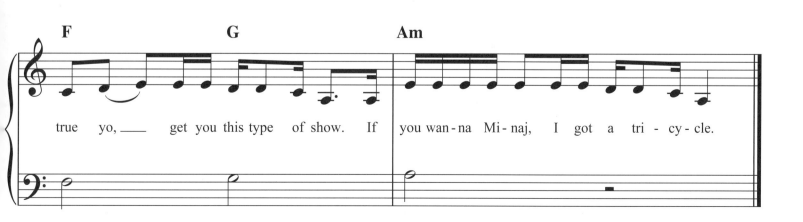

true yo, ____ get you this type of show. If you wan - na Mi - naj, I got a tri - cy - cle.

THANK U, NEXT

Words and Music by ARIANA GRANDE,
VICTORIA McCANTS, KIMBERLY KRYSIUK,
TAYLA PARX, TOMMY BROWN,
CHARLES ANDERSON and MICHAEL FOSTER

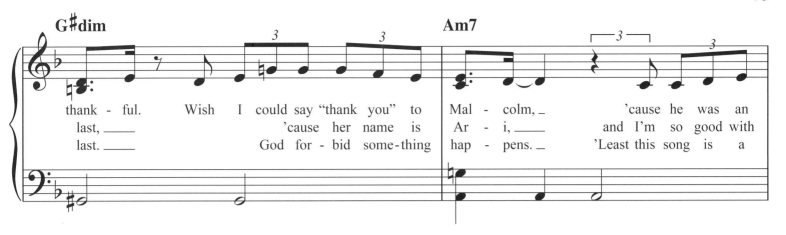

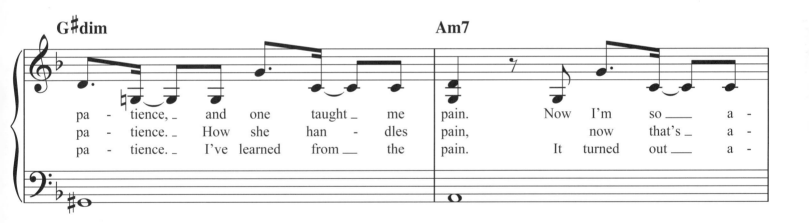

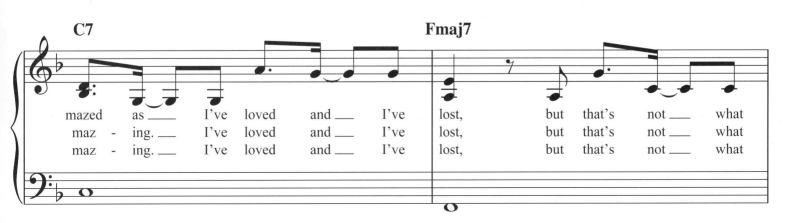

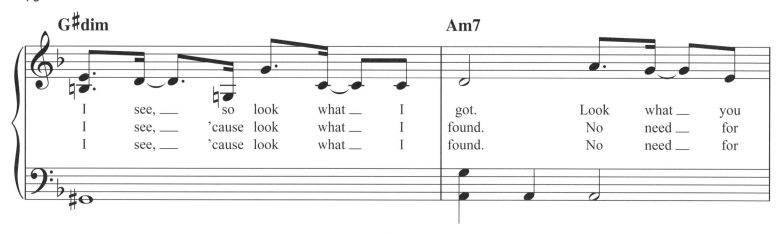

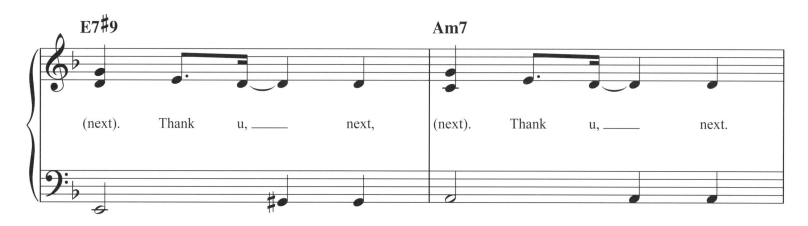

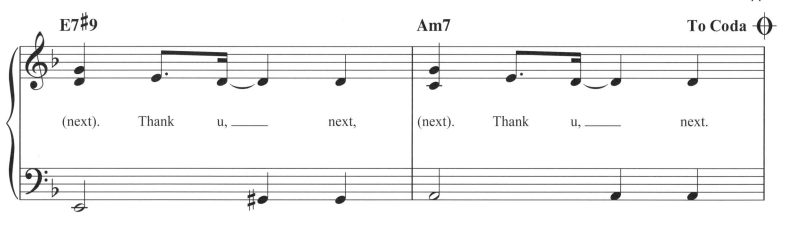

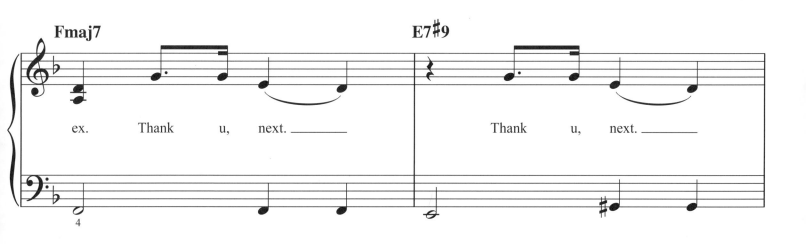

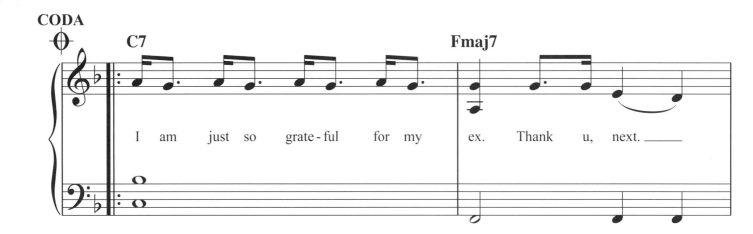

CODA

I am just so grate-ful for my ex. Thank u, next._____

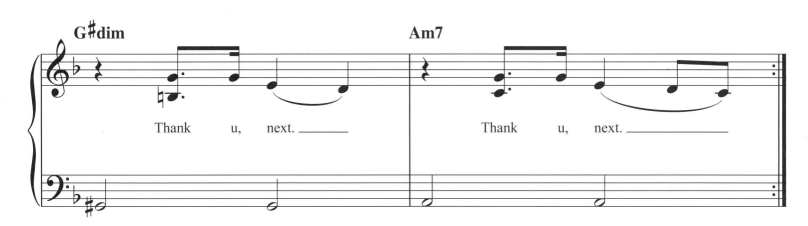

Thank u, next._____ Thank u, next._____

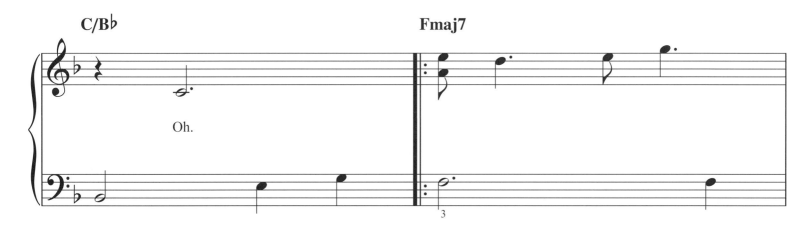

Oh.

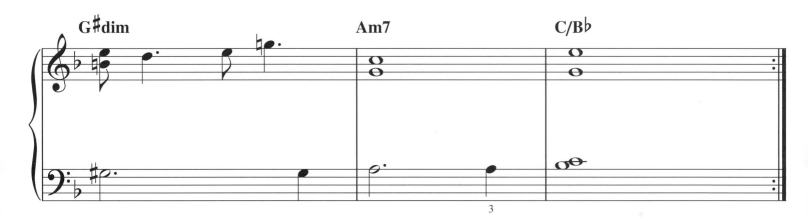

THE WAY

Words and Music by BRENDA GORDON RUSSELL,
HARMONY SAMUELS, AMBER STREETER,
MALCOLM McCORMICK, AL SHERROD LAMBERT
and JORDIN SPARKS

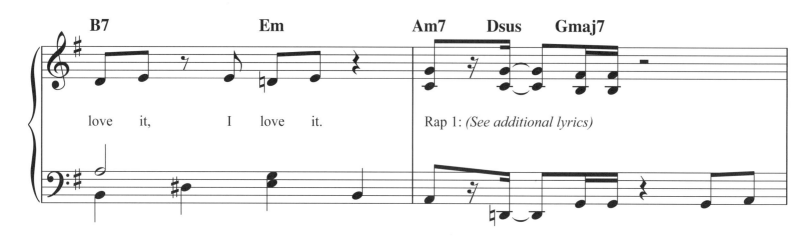

love it,   I love it.   Rap 1: *(See additional lyrics)*

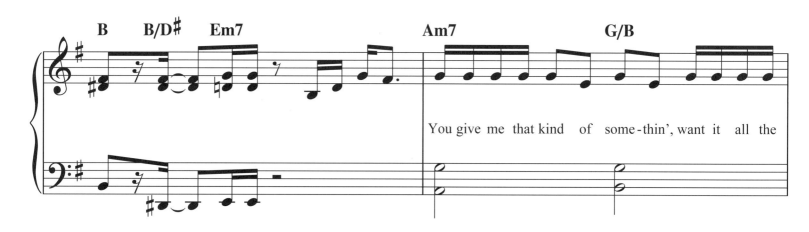

You give me that kind of some-thin', want it all the

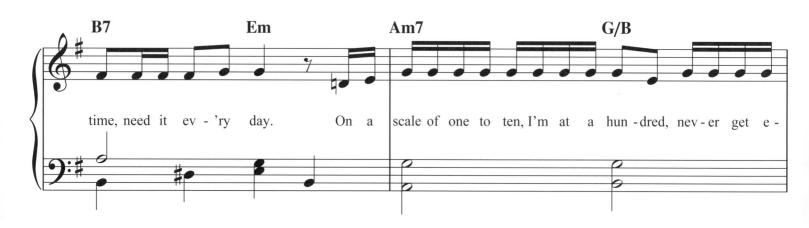

time, need it ev-'ry day.   On a   scale of one to ten, I'm at a hun-dred, nev-er get e-

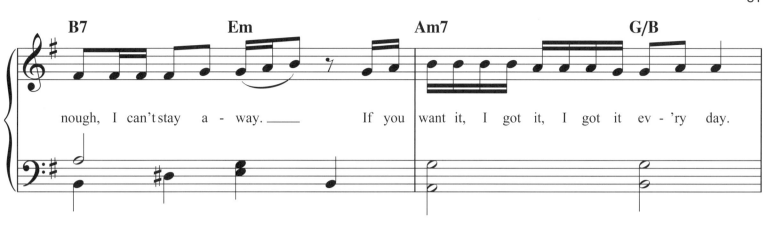

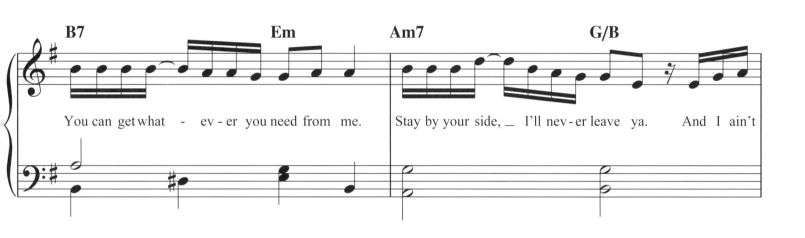

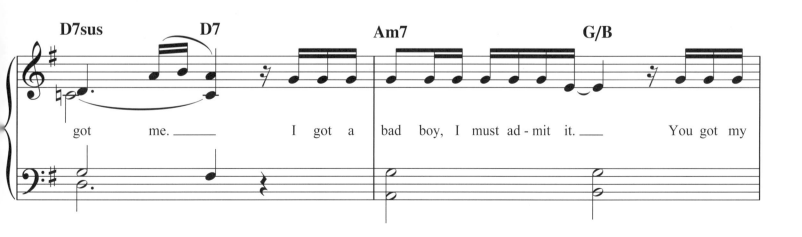

B7　　　　　　　　　　　**Em**　　　**Am7**　　　　　　**G/B**

heart, don't know how you did it. ___　　　And　　I don't care who sees it, babe.　I don't wan - na hide the way I

B7　　　　　　　　　　　**Em**　　　**Am7**　　　　　　**G/B**

feel　when you're next to　me. ___　　　　I　　love　the way ___　you make me feel. ___　I

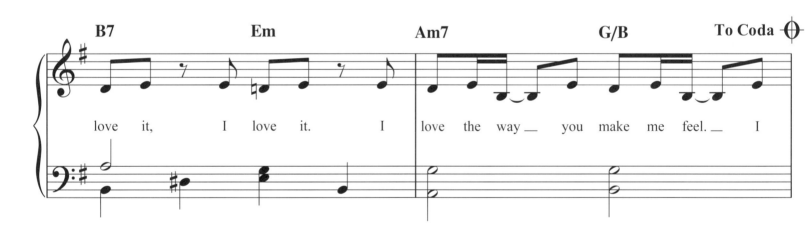

B7　　　　　　　**Em**　　　　**Am7**　　　　　**G/B**　　　　**To Coda** ⊕

love　it,　I　love　it.　I　　love　the way ___　you make me feel. ___　I

B7　　　　　　　**Em**　　　　**Am7**　　　　　**G/B**

love　it,　I　love　it.　　Ooh,　so cra - zy, you get my　heart jump - in'

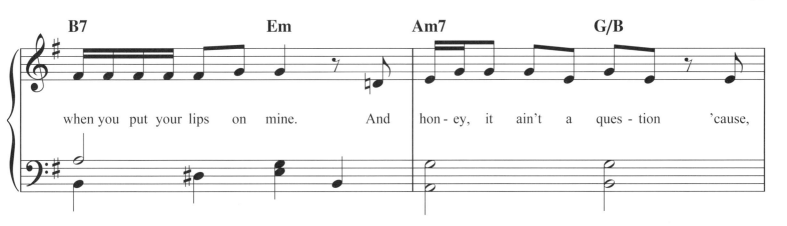

when you put your lips on mine. And hon-ey, it ain't a ques-tion 'cause,

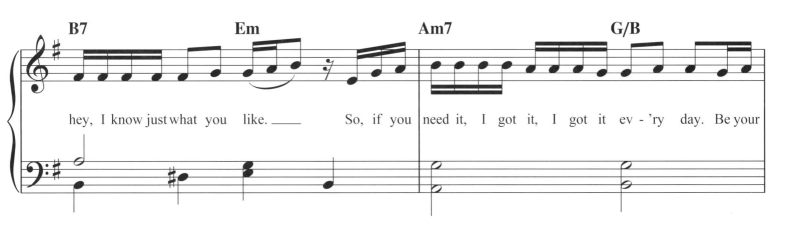

hey, I know just what you like. ____ So, if you need it, I got it, I got it ev-'ry day. Be your

lov-er and friend, _you'll find it all in me. Stay by your side, _ I'll nev-er leave ya. And I ain't

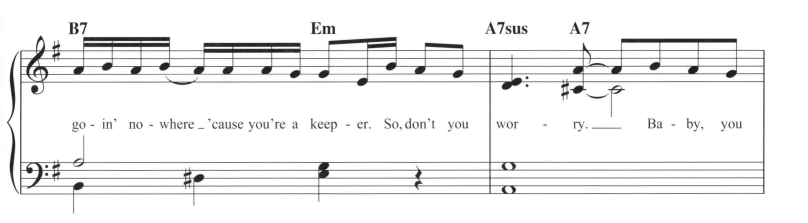

go-in' no-where _'cause you're a keep-er. So, don't you wor - ry. ____ Ba - by, you

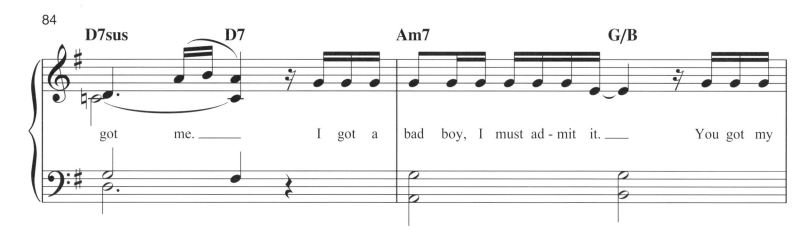

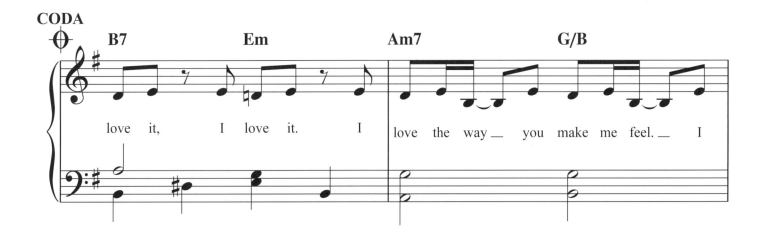

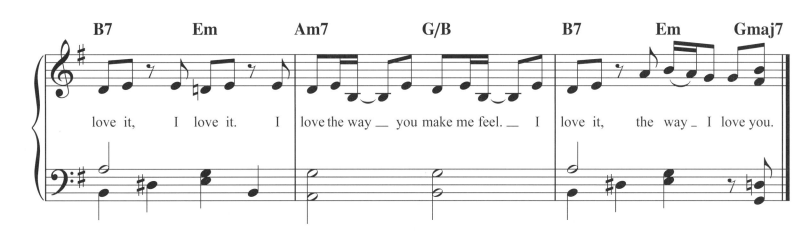

Additional Lyrics

Rap 1: Say, I'm thinking 'bout her every second, every hour
Do my singing in the shower, picking petals off of flowers.
Like, do she love me, do she love me not?
I ain't a player, I just...

Rap 2: Uh, I make you feel so fine, make you feel so fine.
I hope you hit me on my celly when I sneak in your mind.
You a princess to the public, but a freak when it's time.
Said your bed be feeling lonely, so you're sleeping in mine.
Come and watch a movie with me, American Beauty or Bruce Almighty, that's groovy.
Just come and move closer to me. I got some feelings for you I'm not gonna get bored of.
But, baby, you an adventure, so let me come and explore ya.